How F*cked Up Is Your Management?

How F*
Up Is Yo
Manag

Johnathan Nightingale

Melissa Nightingale

cked

our

AN UNCOMFORTABLE
CONVERSATION ABOUT
MODERN LEADERSHIP

ement?

RAW SIGNAL

Published by Raw Signal Press
www.rawsignal.ca
For corporate/event bulk orders, contact press@rawsignal.ca

Deposit, Library and Archives Canada, 2017
ISBN-13: 978-0-9959643-0-3 (paperback)
ISBN-13: 978-0-9959643-1-0 (ebook)

Cover and interior design by Ingrid Paulson

1 2 3 4 5 6 7 8 9 10   21 20 19 18 17

To B & L

Contents

Welcome

Why are you here?

Did someone hand you this book? Maybe one of our blog posts was forwarded to you ages ago and you've followed us since? Maybe you spotted the cover on a shelf and picked it up because you like swears. You're in luck—this book definitely has some swears.

However you found us, we're glad you did. This is not a big book, but it's an important one. We take this stuff seriously. Between us we've seen the insides of dozens of the world's most innovative companies, and the results are bleak. Absentee bosses. Poorly run meetings. Ping pong tables and beer in place of culture. The modern office, with its open floor plans and free snacks, is failing to deliver on the most basic workplace essential: actual management. Even the devoted managers we meet tell us that no one taught them how to do this stuff—they're learning it as they go, and they're terrified that they're fucking it up.

More often than not, they're right. And it doesn't have to be this way.

How to Use This Book

We should start by saying that this isn't an end-to-end book. It's okay if you need to hop around between sections or read the last chapter first. We kept the chapters largely independent of one another to make this easier. There are shared themes, but there's no correct order.

We also expect that at different phases in your career, some of these sections will speak to you more than others, or that some chapters feel like they're written for someone else in your life. That's okay, too.

When a chapter pulls from a post we've written online, we used the same title so it's easy to look up or share with a friend. But some of the stuff in here has never appeared online, and might never. The friends who need to read those chapters will have to buy their own copy, or borrow yours.

Our Origin Myth

The vast majority of this book was written in our living room. We'd take turns writing posts about tech leadership or startup management. Over time, we amassed something of a following. We've been in tech for our entire careers, and, at first, we assumed that was our only audience.

But we quickly learned that folks in other industries were reading, sharing, and commenting, industries in which we'd never worked a day in our lives. They emailed to say it was the first time in a long time they'd understood how to manage their teams, align their organization, or better understand what the heck their boss was thinking. These were people in health care, in agriculture, in law, and in mining. We started to get the sense that our writing wasn't just about leadership in tech or startups, but about leadership in general. It's a humbling thing. It was the first time we started to talk about putting this book together.

This stuff is hard, and it's one of the areas where leaders need the most support but often get the least. When we write, we often think of ourselves a few years ago. We think about what we wish we'd known then, the mistakes we could have avoided, and the successes that would come in time. This book exists because of those comments and emails. If you've ever been unsure about whether to comment on a post you've enjoyed from some stranger's website, now you know. Those comments made us believe there were enough people who gave a shit to make it worth doing. Thanks for giving a shit.

Signal and Noise

There are already a bunch of folks writing about this stuff. In a sense, that's part of the problem. When you don't know what you don't know, everyone out there looks equally credible. Part of our desire to write this stuff down is the gap we see in the writing about startup life and leadership in general.

Social media is chock full of think pieces on management. But so much of what we read there doesn't match our experience. The posts are well written and pithy, the headlines tantalizing, but they don't cover the stuff that happens in our day-to-day. And in some cases they advance theories or propose systems that we don't believe can help *any* company actually succeed.

There is good stuff coming out of some of the writers in the venture capital space. vcs have a rare vantage point: they get to sit on a bunch of boards, hear a bunch of pitches, work with a bunch of entrepreneurs, and do all of it simultaneously. They have access to a wondrous amount of context and, as a result, they tend to be great trendspotters. They write prophetic pieces about the state of the industry and what's to come. They often have great insight on corporate strategy and product growth models. But they rarely touch on how to be a better boss or how to think about the organizational impact of scaling your company. And when they do, it's clear that they are well out of their element.

It feels so different when you actually operate inside a business. The problems you are trying to solve are much more complex when you add humans to the mix. It's no longer a matter of having a crisp vision or a well-articulated strategy. Those things definitely matter, but once you get a large team of people involved, all bets are off. The perfect vision, the defensible strategy—these are nothing if you can't get a group of people fired up about helping you get there. This book is not about strategy; this book is about operating.

What We Mean When We Say "An Uncomfortable Conversation"

We didn't set out to be controversial, but depending on your background and experience, some of what's here may piss you off. A lot of what's in this book is uncomfortable to talk about. We try to confront some messy power dynamics. We definitely disagree with some received wisdom. And a lot of what we have to say now was uncomfortable for us to learn about in the first place. We find that discomfort is generally a good indication of where there's work to do.

Apply what's useful, skip ahead to the chapters that resonate, and double back when something catches your eye. Spend time on what about it gets under your skin. You don't need to agree with everything in this book, but if you disagree, you should ask yourself why. It might be that we're wrong, or that we've said something that doesn't apply in your world. But it might also be that we're right and you just don't like what that implies.

We'd consider it a failure if you made it start to finish through this book without wincing, without having some work to do. As leaders in modern organizations, we all have some work to do.

What We Mean When We Say "Modern Leadership"

We wrote this book to share more of what we learned the hard way. There's a lot that we wish we'd known when we were starting out in tech twenty years ago.

The canon of management classics doesn't have much to say on the management and leadership discussions that are happening right now. If diversity is mentioned at all, closely linked ideas like privilege aren't. Books that talk about how to partner well with HR don't have much to say about the modern trend of start-ups skipping on HR hires altogether. We now have companies crowing about how they're entirely doing away with management. The classics don't have much to say about that idiocy. We are in the midst of a major shift, not only in the age of the modern workforce, but in the expectations people have of businesses, bosses, and corporate accountability.

The fundamentals of leadership haven't changed because *people* haven't changed. Our job as managers and leaders is to make our teams more effective. Our job as humans is to add some compassion to the world and leave it more excellent and just than we found it. Modern leadership is the never-ending work to reconcile and integrate those things. What is different today is that we have access to so many more perspectives and exposure to so much more criticism. Our people expect more from us than the management classics ever anticipated.

That change is exciting for us. We've built our careers on it. But it means the management canon needs an update. What you hold here is what we've learned toward that so far.

ONE
Let's Talk

A series of uncomfortable conversations

/1

How Fucked Up Is Your Management?

A quiz, an extremely boring manifesto, and a free drink coupon

> Johnathan

It's taken me fifteen years in this industry to figure out how to be any good at what I do. I don't know how to write it all down yet, but I'm going to give a piece of it away to you in the next five minutes.

It starts with an observation that is controversial to many folks, even though I think it's like saying that water is wet:

> Managing people is exceptionally hard to do well. People are complex, and organizations are just full of them.

I have managed many people at a variety of scales and worked with leaders of other organizations big and small. I've trained up new managers and watched them grow into strong leaders. I've sat with them through hirings and firings, and watched them struggle with both.

I've had members of my teams get married, get divorced, have kids, lose kids, attempt suicide and (mercifully) fail. I have had an employee die, and to this day the social network birthday reminders gut me. No one who takes management seriously *and* does it well finds this stuff easy. No one who's been at it for very long imagines that there are shortcuts.

But, as P.T. Barnum probably didn't say,

There's a sucker born every minute.

The infatuation with management shortcuts, particularly in startup culture, is rampant. The charitable explanation is that a lot of classic management practice feels slow, and founders are trying to unfetter their people. I think the harsher, truer explanation is that many founders are inexperienced managers and don't understand the trade-offs they're making at their employees' expense.

Let's Try a Quiz

Score 1 "My management culture is fucked up" point for each of the following:

→ We have an unlimited vacation policy.
→ We don't do regular one-on-ones, but we have open office hours or are super available if anyone wants to chat.
→ We don't have a *process* for interviewing—we just hire awesome people when we meet them.

- → We super-care about diversity, but we don't want to lower the bar so we just hire the best person for the job even if it means diversity suffers.
- → We don't have defined levels and career paths for our employees—we're a really flat org.
- → We don't have formal managers for every staff member—everyone just gets their work done.
- → We don't have, like, HR HR, but our recruiter/office manager/only female employee is super good if you want someone to talk to.
- → We don't do performance improvement plans for employees who are struggling. We just have a super-honest conversation about how they aren't a good fit and fire them.
- → We would have some hard explaining to do if our salary list accidentally became public.

I'll cancel out you your first point for free. I'll cancel a second one because it's hard to run a business and there's always something you wish you could get to but haven't yet. I understand that. And, if you're on the bubble, I'll cancel one more if there's a thing on this list you are trying to change.

So how'd your company do? Fewer than 3 points? I'm happy for you and your colleagues. 4? 5?

More?

What a Waste

I've talked to people who score *7s and 8s*. Sometimes they're proud of it.

What I've learned is that a high score on that silly little quiz tells me two not-silly things about you: you're wasting time, and you're wasting your investors' money. And what's extra sad is that you thought you were doing the opposite.

You thought you were saving time by cutting needless process and especially needless meetings. Ugh, *meetings*, right? But a lot of these practices will increase turnover and lower productivity.

You know what costs a lot of time? When good people quit. You lose accumulated knowledge, you take a significant velocity hit, and you often have knock-on morale drag on the staff that stay. One-on-ones take time, but they let people get things off their chest. They also feed motivation and team identity. Defined levels and career paths take work to develop, but they're a straightforward way to give people mastery goals and direction. A well-designed performance improvement plan takes longer than summary dismissal, but it can turn a struggling employee around and lift an entire team's output.

Some of these policies do *seem* to save money. Unlimited vacation can be a useful way to avoid paying out accrued time when employees leave. And not hiring an HR person *does* save you their salary.

But a core value of good management is that your investment in your employees pays off as those investments grow in scope and impact. Well-managed employees make your company better. They mentor new people, take on new skills, and take personal ownership in the quality of their team's work.

Ever look at some company getting it right and think, *"How did they hire all those amazing people?"* I'll tell you how. They *grew* them.

And they retained them. And that attracted more great people. People talk, and that flows both ways. Skimping on your people is a foolish (and gross) way to save money.

Don't Take My Word for It

I try to manage well and thoughtfully, but there is certainly no shortage of disagreement out there on the right way to run things.

Valve software's culture doc is near-biblical for many folks, yet it garners a pretty high score on my test. Valve makes more money than I do, and better games, too; maybe they're right? I don't know. Former Valve folk are not gentle with their description of a culture that "felt like high school," with implicit favor-based power structures operating behind the scenes. I don't want to work in that kind of place. Maybe you do?[1]

Remember when GitHub was so proud of how they didn't really bother with traditional management? Somehow, even with their unlimited paid time off, it didn't go well.[2]

I hear they're hiring more managers now, and I'm hopeful for them. My hope is not that they feel beaten and subjugated and pay their Manager Tax. My hope is that they realize how harmful their hubris is to the employees who helped them build such a central piece of the technology landscape.

An Extremely Boring Manifesto

Look, management may be hard, but this test is pretty easy to pass. And it proceeds from the first rule of startup club:

The First Rule of Startup Club: If you're not planning to be the best in the world at something other people already do well, then don't mess around with implementing your own version of it. Use theirs.

We usually cite this in reference to databases, or unit test harnesses, or snack providers. But it's just as true here.

I don't need you to be the best in the world at management. But if you're not planning to be, if you're not going to be really studious and dedicated to it, then for God's sake stop messing with it. I promise you you can't build a better management system in your spare time. Instead,

→ Set up every employee with a clear direct manager, and expect them to hold regular one-on-ones. Discuss their current work, but also their goals and development.

→ Be clear about every role or, if you can't manage that, at least about every role with multiple people in it. Define the expectations of the role and where it's headed. Employees should know which level or role they're in.

→ Set salaries according to role and calibrate against your market (your HR person can help here).

→ Have a basic process for sourcing and interviews.[3] Eliminate bias where you can. Interview for well-defined roles so that you know what your salary range is, and don't get anchored by savvy candidates who manipulate the offer phase.

→ Give people benefits and vacation time that make them feel loved and help them be excellent without exploding your burn rate. Make sure they take that vacation.

It's stupefying to me, but if you do those things, you'll be head and shoulders above many of your peers in the industry. You'll be able to attract and retain talent better. Your employees will grow and take on broader leadership roles. Word will get around that your company is run by grown-ups.

What's even more amazing to me is this: **Most people won't do it.** Most people will still try to shortcut things and then wonder aloud why they can't find great people. They'll conclude that they need to pay higher salaries because their people keep fleeing. They'll miss targets, they'll fail, and they'll explain that startup is just *super* hard and maybe they were just too early.

Like most manifestos, this one's easier to read than it is to live. I understand that business is full of conflicting tensions and priorities. But if you can't do these things, these *table-stakes things*, then I need you to seriously consider the possibility that running an organization is not for you. Find a cofounder who gets this stuff. Hire and empower leaders to operate your company while you stick to the ideas and get out of their way. *Something.* These are people's lives you're dealing with. If I sound irate, that's why.

And to those of you out there who do understand this, who lead with purpose, clarity, and empathy: **I see you.** You are heroes who don't get enough credit. And if you're ever in Toronto, your first drink is on me.

/2

Why It's a Mistake to Be a Startup Superhero

An appealing job that you don't want

> Melissa

You might not know it to look at me, but I am a startup superhero.

If you saw me walking on the street downtown, your eyes would probably bounce right off of me. I'm pretty Clark Kent these days—right down to my hip square glasses.

But deep in my closet, behind stacks of skinny jeans and branded hoodies, I've got a cape. On the back, in big yellow letters, it says STARTUP SUPERHERO. And then in tiny white letters underneath it says *look out*.

Well, I guess technically I'm a retired startup superhero.

It's been ages since I suffered from startup superhero martyrdom, but it's a condition I'm deeply familiar with. I know the seductive siren song of problems only *you* can solve, 3 a.m. emails only *you* can respond to but that definitely need a response right at that moment. I know all about the frenetic task-swapping that is so easily confused for progress but is, sadly, just running in place.

This is the story of how I hung up my cape and discovered my true superpowers.

Let's start at the beginning.

◆ ◆ ◆

It's 2000. I'm working at my first startup. I don't have a good sense of where work stops and where my social life begins. My coworkers are my friends. Or, at least, I *think* they're my friends. It's hard to tell because it's been so long since I've hung out with anyone else.

I'm in the office six or seven days a week. I eat breakfast with my team. I eat lunch with my team. I often don't leave the office until after midnight. But I don't really mind because these are the concessions you make when you're changing the world and planning to become a millionaire all at the same time. It's a lot to juggle.

We have big aspirations. The internet is new—it doesn't feel as new as it is. We're early to an idea that won't have legs for another five or six years at least. We talk about the *democratization of media*. We talk about *citizen journalism*. We talk about *removing the gatekeepers*. We talk about *giving voices to the voiceless*. We talk about media, streaming, and user-generated content.

We have the urgency of our disruptive vision but lack important conditions of the strategy needed to fulfill it. We are right but we are way too early. Smartphones will unlock so much of the future we envision, but they are still a ways away.

Five years in the future, another company with a similar disruptive vision will come onto the scene. They are a tiny little operation called YouTube. You may have heard of them.

But in the meantime, A16 is happening in DC to protest the International Monetary Fund and World Bank annual meetings. This is right after the 1999 Battle of Seattle protests around the World Trade Organization Ministerial Conference. The anti-globalization movement is starting to gain steam. It's about a decade before the G20 Summit protests in Toronto.

We have camera equipment. We have a website. We have branded T-shirts. We have laminated press badges *that we made*. And we have moxie.

The day before the A16 protests, there's a demonstration against the prison industrial complex. It's April 15, 2000. Our startup's office is within walking distance of the protest so we grab the camera gear and head up there to see what's happening. We set up our cameras alongside CNN and the local affiliates. We get into fights with seasoned Betamax veterans because they try to block our shots or move our tripods. We hold our ground. Our branded T-shirts say "The Whole World Is Watching" across the front. Our URL is across the back. We wear them without irony.

Two of us break away from the main protest and go in search of a better shot. We want to be *above* the protest. We look around. It's downtown DC—the only way to be above is to get access to one of the surrounding office buildings. Lucky for us, it's a Saturday.

We approach the janitorial crew of a building right in the middle of the demonstration. We ask if we can film from a few floors up. We offer one of them a spare branded T-shirt. He seems to think this is a pretty good deal and lets us in. The office is mostly empty and no one is there to tell the cleaning crew that letting strangers with cameras into your office building is a quick way to get fired in Washington.

From above, we can see everything. A photographer is already set up. We position our tripod next to her.

We are filming when the police begin mass arrests below. We stop filming when plainclothes FBI agents enter the building and ask to see our IDs. We show them our homemade laminated press badges. The photographer next to us shows them her *Washington Post* press credentials.

They demand to see ID.

The *Washington Post* photog refuses. We refuse.

They demand again. They say we will be arrested if we don't comply.

The *Washington Post* photog complies. We comply.

They take our licenses and write down the details. They tell us to vacate the building but that we are free to go. We are careful not to get picked up by the police. We walk back to the office.

The *Washington Post* photographer is not so lucky.

Shortly after we all leave that building, she is detained and arrested. While watching the news that night, we learn she is Carol Guzy, a Pulitzer Prize–winning journalist.

Some of our startup employees get caught up in the mass arrests and are detained. Our camera gear is held by police while we're waiting for the employees to be processed. It's chaos. I feel the hum of adrenaline under my skin while I dial the number for DC Central Booking. I inquire about my missing coworkers, but, alas, there's no record of anyone by those names. They haven't been entered into the system yet. They haven't been charged with any crime. They are still waiting... on buses, handcuffed, for hours. It's starting to get dark. I need to rescue them.

I go back to the office and keep calling Central Booking but to no avail. Later, as part of a class action lawsuit, we will learn that this was intentional, a tactic meant to distract and confuse protesters.

A couple of us stay at the office in case our coworkers are released. In case they call. In case there's bail to be made. In case we need to go get the cameras. In case they need us.

It's late and I'm tired so I tip over a box of giant branded T-shirts. They are all men's larges. It's 2000. It will be many years before we get more than just men's L and XL shirts.

I pile the shirts under my head and stretch out my legs on the office floor. I am curled up, in a pile of white Hanes shirts, when the morning sun glares through the windows of our Dupont Circle office.

◆ ◆ ◆

There is so much nostalgia in this story. I'm smiling while writing it, remembering a time when I was that young, that idealistic, that green. Sometimes it feels like large parts of my life happened to someone else—me, but a different me somehow. Other times I feel like I've lived several lives consecutively, with just the one me but with a narrative that writes itself like rings on a tree trunk.

In the intro, I promised that this wasn't me just telling tales around the campfire from the first dotcom boom. That this was a fable, a story with a lesson at the end.

These are lessons I have had to learn many times in my career before they finally stuck. And still, I work at them.

If you are secretly wearing tighty whities over leggings under your skinny jeans, this is for you.

Know Where Your Work Stops and Your Social Life Begins

Tech is particularly good at creating the conditions that normalize this blurry line. Between booze in the office, drinks after work, offsites, outings, and all-hands meetings, it can feel like a bunch of your social needs are well covered during working hours.

In the best version, your colleagues are all fun and awesome people you'd hang out with even if you weren't being paid. They're the kind of people you'd go have a couple drinks with. They are the people you'd sit around playing board games with until 2 a.m. It's nice to like your coworkers. No one is saying you can't have nice things. But...

If you can't point to downtime that is separate and distinct from your uptime, you are at dire risk of burnout, and there's a really good chance you need to set better boundaries.

Go Home

The part of the story where I tip over a box of T-shirts into a make-shift bed like I'm some sort of feral cat? Please!

That entire episode would have happened exactly the same way if I'd slept at home in my own bed, on my own sheets, with my own pillow. No one needed me to sleep on the office floor. Hell, no one even *asked* me to stay in the office overnight. I did that— just me, myself, and my big ol' martyr complex.

At no point were DC police playing by the rules. The eventual charge they laid on the protesters was something ridiculous like "parading without a permit." Me sleeping in the office did not hasten the release of my colleagues. Me sleeping in the office probably hastened the back issues that older me is grumpy about.

Have a Plan for Theoretical Emergencies. Execute the Plan for Actual Ones.

The number of times the "in case" scenarios that showed up in my superhero rationale actually came to fruition? Zero. None of the "in case" scenarios actually happened.

Scenario drills are an important part of emergency response training, but there's a reason scenario creation or invention isn't done as part of active emergency response. In an actual emergency, you need the plan to work when the context changes. For the above story, having a plan would look something like this:

Before sending staff out into a DC protest with expensive camera equipment and in the days of few cellphones, gather said staff in a conference room. Some person, presumably some adultish person who is in charge, stands up and says, "If we get separated, everyone meet back at the office. If you need help, here's the one number to call. Write it on your arm in Sharpie. Person who is on phone duty, you stay at the office. Answer the phone if someone calls. Go home once you have seen everyone who was out and all the cameras are safely back in the office."

Hang up your cape and lock the door on your way out.

/3

You Won't Brilliant Your Way out of This

How smart people turn into mid-level plateau jackasses

> Johnathan

I'm gonna make this one quick, because I know you've got a lot going on.

You're not as smart as you think you are.

Don't get me wrong—you're smart. You have good, creative ideas that are well connected to the way the business works. Those smarts have helped you climb out of the junior ranks early. You stand out because your ideas are surprising and cut across a broad swath of the business. You interview well, especially with executives who feel like they need to inject some new energy.

So now you're operating at a more senior level. You've picked up a few direct reports, though they're junior and sort of slow. You don't expect much of them other than output. As for the rest of the org, what really surprises you now that you have more access is how *dumb* everyone else is. How slow they are. How much better you could do their job.

If this sounds familiar, you're in trouble. And it will get worse for you before it gets better. It's fixable, but the skills that got you into this mess can't get you out of it.

The Making of a Jackass

Here's what went down that you didn't notice.

When you were junior in your role, someone more senior spotted your brilliance. My hunch is that you come from a lot of privilege already, as women and minorities rarely get that same opportunity.[1] But either way, you got your chance to speak up, someone bet on your ideas, and it worked! I love that part—your ideas are great.

That success put you in a different box. You got talked about as *really promising. Going places. Super smart.* People gave you opportunities to take on new, meaty work and you knocked them down. And that fed your internal notion that you were indeed *super smart*, and that other people weren't.

That attitude shows. People got hurt and frustrated and shut out. But while you were still protected by the people elevating you, it worked out okay. They came in and cleaned after you messed things up. The results spoke for themselves, and reflected well on your managers. Those managers were willing to take some collateral damage.

You didn't see this. You probably even started to think you were cleverer than the people elevating you. But your early success would not have been possible without them.

No More Parachute

Act II is a lot harder. Now you're more senior. You have the title you wanted, though you share it with *lesser* people. You're still smart, still have great ideas, but nothing seems to *happen* with them anymore.

This is usually when you (and I've met several of you along the way) decide to get into politics. You try to play people off against each other. *You start shit.* Some people fall for it, but most of them see it coming. They compare notes. And whereas before, you were getting streamlined into every high-visibility project, people now try to steer around you. They've learned that adding you to a project makes it 300% smarter but gross.

Maybe you're fired, but one way or another you eventually leave.

Interviewing is easy for you; it's not hard to find your next thing. The first couple of projects go really well. But then that friction shows up again. You try to game your way through, but still everyone is so *slow*, so bad at their jobs. You bounce off that gig, too.

And the next one.

And the next one.

The Unmaking of a Jackass

Tech is weird. When Gary Vaynerchuk says "Ideas are shit, execution's the game,"[2] most tech leaders agree. I know I do. But then many of those people go back to their companies and hire ideas people. They seem genuinely surprised when this doesn't work out well. I don't honestly know what to tell them when that happens.

As for you, you need to start keeping score on execution, not ideas. It's a hard change, abandoning the scoring system that inevitably puts you on top, but it's the only way out. You'll know you're getting there when you start to realize how *much* some of those people, those *slow* people, get done. I've seen this happen when people start their own companies and there's no idiot CEO or executive to blame. I've also seen it happen when something happens in life that sees them brought low.

It comes down to this: Find a way to be humbled.

On the other side of a gut-wrenching dose of humility, change can be complete and permanent. You recognize that the only road to high-output execution is to bring others along. Force of ideas won't do that, but it can be the secret sauce that makes you great once the team believes in you.

This wasn't my particular pathology, so I can't speak from personal experience about how that change feels. I can only tell you what I've seen. One consistent characteristic I've seen in people who make this change is that they're mortified by how they used to behave. Another consistent trait I've seen is that they start racking up regular, unmitigated success.

How's that for a good idea?

/4

Why It's a Mistake to Hire Superheroes
If Spider-Man shows up, tell him the job has been filled

> Melissa

Welcome to startup interview #27.

In our opening scene, the curtain lifts on a startup conference room. There's a big monitor on the wall. There's a brightly painted accent wall behind the monitor. The Aeron chairs are tucked neatly under the reclaimed wood table. The minimalist vibe is pleasant, even a little familiar.

You, the hiring manager, are getting excited. After a parade of people who are either too corporate, too junior, too senior, or not right for the role, you finally have what seems like a viable candidate.

You are struck by your candidate's deep commitment to their last gig. As they talk about their work, you write down words like *diligent*, *dedicated*, and *passionate*. They have a can-do attitude that stands out, especially in a startup context.

You want people who are willing to trade predictability and stability for an opportunity to define their own path. You are looking for self-starters, hires who are comfortable with a high degree of ambiguity. You want blank canvas types, not cogs.

So you ask questions that test for that superhuman skill set. You want to know about a time when they built a program or department from scratch. You want to hear about how they crushed it in their last job. You romanticize the all-nighters, and your adrenaline pulses every time they punctuate a story with "It was crazy times."

You aren't concerned about burnout and breakdowns and shouting matches and turf wars. We're all adults here, right?

The Honeymoon Period

Here's the thing: At first, it's awesome to have a superhero on board. They hit the ground running, and many of the things that originally sold you on the candidate in the interview process show up in spades over those first few months. Your superhero tackles problems with an intensity and energy that's unlike anything you've seen before.

You have a major project on the horizon. Maybe a software launch, maybe a new product—it doesn't really matter, so long as it's **big** and **important** and **mission critical**. This is exactly what your superhero says they want when you talk about what's next in your weekly one-on-ones.

The skills that shone so brightly in the first few months seem promising. They have proven they can deliver on small, single-threaded initiatives. They have earned your trust. Now it's time to step it up. You put your superhero on your massive project.

After a couple of weeks, red flags start to emerge. Those things that seemed so promising in the interview—the passion, dedication, and diligence—start to take an ugly turn.

All Hell Breaks Loose

Your superhero is used to being a lone wolf. While they excel in a purely individual contributor role, the moment you need them to play well with others, all hell breaks loose. The superhero gets in fights in meetings and complains in one-on-ones about how stupid all the other teams are, how they don't understand the business, how they aren't as passionate, dedicated, or diligent.

Your superhero doesn't ask for input. They don't check in at milestones. When you raise this in one-on-ones, they tell you that you don't need to worry. They're on it. They can do it all. They will put in the hours. They will pull all-nighters if they need to.

And suddenly it drops.

You're transported back to that refreshingly minimalist conference room with the modern take on midcentury modern lines. It's clear to you now. The interview, the "crazy times," the intensity, the frenetic energy, the 3 a.m. emails that could easily have happened during business hours, the procrastination, the finger pointing.

You haven't hired someone who thrives in chaos.
You've hired someone who *sows* chaos.
Shit.

What You Should Have Asked

If you'd listened a bit closer or asked the right questions, you would have surfaced several problem areas that are closely coupled with the superhuman skills you seek: a marked distrust for peers, a discomfort with teamwork, and the trail of bodies where that energy shifts from being a positive force to being a toxic one.

In the "oh shit" moment when you realize that the "thrives in chaos" keys are right next to the "creates chaos" keys on the startup employee cliché keyboard of life—you can see it clearly. And come to think of it, when you did the reference checks, you actually heard quite a bit that indicated Stormy Waters Ahead. But you were pretty far into an interview process at that point, everyone you'd met prior to your superhero was a dud, and that req had been open for a long time. And, if you're being totally honest with yourself, you worried that the headcount was going to evaporate if it didn't get closed. And, and, and.

There were signs. There are *always* signs. But you didn't want to see them.

You asked about big projects and taking them from concept to completion. You failed to ask for examples of times when your superhero worked cross-functionally.

You asked about what they've done. You failed to ask who did the work, how, and when.

You failed to register that what should have been a narrative with a colorful cast of characters was a monologue with a single lead playing all the key roles, like some sort of startup Eddie Murphy movie.

You heard the stories about urgency and freneticism. You failed to push on the root causes for that urgency, where it was a result of the business and where it was a construct of our superhero.

You called references but you asked yes-or-no questions about how your superhero did in their last job. You didn't ask direct reports if they'd work for them again. You failed to ask managers if they'd hire them again.

Now What?

You hired a superhero because the good in the interview seemed so good. And now you have a superhero in your midst and the bad is a problem. A *big* problem. There's a really good chance you'll need to fire them.

Free of your superhero, your team will begin to coalesce. Your cross-functional troubles will dissipate. Your seemingly Herculean efforts will be just another Tuesday.

And in their next interview, your superhero will tell tales about how crazy it was and how urgent and how many all-nighters they pulled. And when you eventually get that reference call, what will you say?

/5

That Time You Failed to Follow Up on Diversity
The space between caring and
not giving a fuck
> Melissa

Remember that time you got all excited and fired up about addressing diversity in tech? Remember how you planned to ride in on your horse and save us all? The implication was that diversity is a problem with a clear solution that the rest of us just haven't been clever enough to spot. That is, until you and that horse came along...

I remember when you misspoke at a company-wide event. Your staff complained that you were out of touch. You wrote to me, embarrassed, close to an internal mutiny. You said you were serious, you wanted to make changes and be a better ally.

Shame Is a Powerful Yet Fleeting Motivator
You told me that you weren't opposed to more women or minorities in tech. You thought that all seemed swell. You felt that the people who had called you out for putting your foot in your mouth were being overly harsh, very unfair.

You asked for advice about how to support greater diversity in tech. I grimaced.

Being asked for free labor to educate people who already enjoy incredible privilege is part of the problem. It feels an awful lot like supporting the busted system that created that lack of diversity in the first place.

But fine. I care about this stuff. I bit my tongue. I dusted off my favorite links of things people who are trying to get smarter about diversity should read.[1] I sent them along and offered to connect again if you had questions.

And you, in this moment of eager fix-it-ness, expressed gratitude and said that of course, you'd follow up.

Except you didn't. You still haven't. And you won't.

Not because you didn't start with a good intention (see Chapter 29). Not exactly because you don't care about diversity. It's just that life got busy. And your calendar is full. And diversity work is somehow different than regular work.

And this is how the patriarchy wins.

Diversity Is Not an Extracurricular Activity

For many startups, diversity efforts are like intramural sports—participation is optional, and if you flake, no biggie. And just like that Ultimate Frisbee team you planned to join in college but didn't, it doesn't hurt your GPA to opt out of diversity work. At least not in ways that you can see right now.

So let's talk about those things that you can't see.

Let's talk about this continuing nonsense about the pipeline problem (see Chapter 10). About how there aren't enough diverse candidates applying to your roles. Or enough internal folks who qualify for those merit-based promotions (Chapter 6).

Let's talk about Uber.[2] Again? Yes, again.[3] And then let's enjoy a collective navel gaze at sxsw, where we wonder aloud how this keeps happening.[4]

Let's talk about the biggest elephant in the room—the one where we accept the broken, fucked-up system that we ask women and people of color to endure. And then we extend it. Not through a small handful of misogynistic bros who want to talk about the developer with the fine ass. Rather, by the complacency of people who would otherwise swear up and down about how they are making the world a better place. How they would love to help the cause, roll up their sleeves, and put in the work.

If only they could find the time.

How You Use Your Time Is How You Prioritize

If you or your organization cannot find the time for diversity work, it's not important to you. It's not because you are jazzed about it but because you're super busy.

If you fail to follow up in favor of more compelling, more pressing, or otherwise more urgent work, you don't care about diversity. And it is only from a place of marked privilege that one can deprioritize the righting of an inequitable system.

If you say you want to help and then fail to follow up, that's worse than not reaching out in the first place. Don't feign interest and passion after getting called out only to lose focus after the dust settles.

If you care, you need to care all the time. Not only on Hallmark holidays. Not only when you fuck up and someone notices. And not only when you hire your first female partner. *All. The. Time.*

Diversity and inclusion are hard work, tiring work. And, too often, thankless work. The people who are doing this work day in, day out are disproportionately the people harmed by our collective lack of progress.

I've written before about my own failings on this front (see Chapter 7). So has my co-author (Chapter 6). We talk openly and painfully about the times we fell on our faces. We put the words out into the world even though it's embarrassing.

Waking up to and owning your own privilege doesn't happen overnight. Fucking up can be a powerful first step in making changes.

But only if you stick with it.

/6

Some Garbage I Used to Believe about Equality

If I'm going to embarrass myself, I'm taking you with me

> Johnathan

I will probably spend the rest of my life trying to be less of an ass. I think this is a fine occupation for most people. But if you, like me, are a straight white man, my encouragement is that you try harder than most.

We have not distinguished ourselves lately, gentlemen. Even our attempts to be better often mess things up. We lurch into complex social discussions offering "Why don't we just..." as an answer. We write articles telling women, without irony, to just try to be more like men if they want to get ahead.[1] Yes. That happens.

In general we are an embarrassment. It would be funny if it weren't so constantly terrifying.

Not All Men

And I know. I know. *You're* not a grotesque and evil bigot. *You* didn't vote for Trump. It hurts to try so hard to be a good guy[2] only to have someone paint you with the same brush as frat house idiots. I have felt that way, too. And it *does* hurt. But two things to consider before we get started:

→ **There's still work for you to do. There always is.** Take the complaints you hear in that context. Complaining about your hurt feelings makes the conversation all about you again. A conversation about the problems women face with sexism *isn't about your feelings*. A conversation about the problems people of color face with racism *isn't about your feelings*. Don't make it about your feelings. It's hard, I know. It's *hard work* to listen through a critique that you feel is unfair to get to the thing at the heart of it that matters. Do the hard work.

→ **Being painted with an unfair, overgeneralized brush is something other folks deal with every damned day.** Every day they are treated differently (mostly worse) than you are because they aren't you. They are told to change who they are to be more like you. That keeps happening.[3] And you are going to go into that conversation and make it about you? Really? *Again?*

I have no standing to tell a person of color what they should do to survive our culture. I don't know what it's like to be a woman in tech (see Chapter 7). Or disabled, or queer, or an immigrant. But I know what it's like to be a straight white guy in tech. I have lived *that* experience. And I know how embarrassing a lot of my own past beliefs have been.

So I'm going to talk about that. And in case you still believe any of these things, I'm gonna try to help scrub them off of your brain.

I promise it'll make you a better leader. I strongly suspect it will make you a better human, too.

I Used to Believe in Meritocracies

This one feels far away now, but I remember it. I remember how much I wanted it to be true. Calling your group a "meritocracy" solidifies your own status as earned (*You have merit!*) and absolves you of discriminatory guilt (*Other people with merit will succeed to the same degree*). A meritocracy sounds like a nice thing. **But the world has never seen that beast.** And it sure as shit isn't in *your* organization.

When you call yourself a "meritocracy," what I hear is ignorance. At this point I have to believe it's deliberate. Mitch and Freada Kapor put it clearly:

If you are a woman or a person of color in tech, hearing a powerful gatekeeper deny that your color or gender (or both) has been a major factor in how you've been treated flies in the face of evidence and experience.[4]

The way we score merit is full of assumptions that work better for some groups than others. Meritocracies say "your GitHub is your resumé." Then they act surprised that their candidate pool doesn't include a lot of single moms without time to hack on hobby projects.

Meritocracies say all that matters is the work. And then Sarah Sharp walks away from a position of considerable "merit" saying,

I finally realized that I could no longer contribute to a community where I was technically respected, but I could not ask for personal respect … I did not want to work professionally with people who were allowed to get away with subtle sexist or homophobic jokes.[5]

I was a senior member of Mozilla, one of the largest, most successful open source communities around. We even had a female founder, Mitchell Baker, who is one of the most formidable people I've met. And still our "meritocracy" was full of people who looked an awful lot like me. And still people solved disagreements by tearing each other apart because *what mattered were the ideas*. I know that, today, their leaders care a lot about this and are working to change it. I'm hopeful for Mozilla, always. But I stopped using the word *meritocracy* a long time ago, and so should you.

I Used to Ask, "Is That Really Gendered/Racist?"

Someone would tell me a story about getting treated poorly or being passed over or misunderstood. They'd tell me it was discriminatory. And I would ask that question, that naive question. Because to me it wasn't obvious. People have treated *me* poorly. People have misunderstood *me*. Why does it always have to be about race? Why does it always have to be about sexism?

Because it always is.

Yes, people of color can screw up for reasons having nothing to do with their color. Yes, women can make mistakes without it being a gender issue. Those things are possible. So you ask this question that feels benign and curious to you. But it's not benign and curious to *them*. Patient folks from underrepresented groups have reinforced this over and over for me until finally I got it.

To someone who isn't straight and white and male and able-bodied and born locally, this question is the latest in a very long line of people doubting your experience.

It is hard to let this into your brain. You want to be able to have an intellectual conversation about it. But instead you just became part of the pile-on of doubt and undercutting. In that broader context, your casual intellectual challenge is part of the same aggressive suppression that follows those people everywhere. You are part of the problem.

You're going to shake your head solemnly at reports that black men get racially profiled by police, and then challenge your black colleague who tells you his last performance review felt biased? Really? Why?

Because it's technically possible that this instance wasn't? Because you want to assume the best of his manager? Assuming the best of people is something you *get* to do because you haven't been kicked in the gut. This shit has been happening for your colleague's whole fucking life. He knows what it is. How about assuming the best of him and his judgment of the situation?

How about believing a woman who says that your colleague harassed her, even though you think he's a good guy? Where's *her* benefit of the doubt?

There's a lot of benefit to that doubt. It can entrench those with power or it can balance the scales. You get to decide where it goes. When you're making that call, err on the side of the people whose balance is light.

I Used to Ask People to Explain Why I Was Wrong

In the real world, there is more than just us. In the real world, the person who's challenged us on something we've said has done us a favor. But our ego is bruised because we *think* we're really quite woke. So we ask her to explain why what we've done is a problem— partly because we want to learn, partly because we want to dispute the charges.

She doesn't owe us that. *We're* the ones who screwed up. **The hard work of understanding what happened and how we should do better is on *us*.** She might help us get there or she might not. But understand that there are vast numbers of us out there screwing up, getting called on it, demanding a free education. A lot of us get that free education, too, despite the immense amount of unpaid labor it represents.

Engage with the syllabus. If you don't know where to start, Lauren Parker has done some more free work for you already.[6]

I've Still Got a Long Way to Go, and So Do You

Anil Dash is right: there are no good guys.[7] There's just trying to do better than you have done.

One thing I always worry about when I write about this stuff is that it re-centers another white straight dude and his perspective. That's why this chapter is addressed to the one group I feel I can legitimately speak to. Even still, I'm no expert on anything except the places where I've personally screwed up. If you recognize some of those screw-ups, I hope I have your attention.

When I'm trying to get better at something, I find it helpful to fill my Twitter feed with it. If you do, too, I'll close with a list of the people who have taught me the most through their work. I find it uncomfortable to follow them sometimes. You should follow them, too.

→ Shanley Kane (@shanley)
→ Joanne McNeil (@jomc)
→ Kronda (@kronda)
→ Ashe Dryden (@ashedryden)
→ EricaJoy (@ericajoy)
→ Marco Rogers (@polotek)
→ Ijeoma Oluo (@ijeomaoluo)
→ Anil Dash (@anildash)
→ Freada Kapor Klein (@therealfreada)
→ Saadia Muzaffar (@thistechgirl)

When you're done following them, get some of your straight white male friends to do the same. That will also be hard work. So do some hard work.

/7

The Tech *Mechitza*
Thoughts on tech's great gender divide
and my experience living on both sides of it
> Melissa

It's fall. It's officially sweater weather in Toronto. Outside the sky is bright and blue and brilliant, but I'm not fooled: winter is coming. Before it does, we get this amazing season where everything changes colors and the city tries to take in the last bit of good weather.

Fall has always been one of my favorite seasons. I don't really enjoy hot weather (a byproduct of a decade in San Francisco). I love when the temperature breaks and the air turns crisp. For someone who spent a long time without distinct seasons, it's a bit like living in a world of pumpkin spice, flannel, and those oversized Roots scarves.

Fall also brings the Jewish high holidays, which these days are really the only time I find myself in synagogue. Maybe it's because so much of the past couple months have been go go go, but given the opportunity to slow down and reflect, my brain does funny things.

Lately, I've Found Myself Thinking about the *Mechitza*

A *mechitza* is the divider that separates the men's and women's sections in Orthodox synagogues. Men sit with men. Women sit with women. In my least favorite version, the women sit upstairs, the men downstairs. I also dislike the ones that split across the room with men at the front and women at the back, behind a wall.

At my dad's shul (synagogue) the men and women sat parallel with a half-height wall between them. When I was six, my mom found and joined a Conservative shul and Dad continued to go to the Orthodox one. We kids got to pick where we wanted to go on weekends.

Going to shul as a girl with Dad meant sitting with the men. This was likely good, though unintentional, preparation for my future career in tech. I have frequently been the only female interview candidate, the only woman on the team, and sometimes the only woman in the company.

I find myself unable to shake this idea of the *mechitza*, this physical representation of gender divide. Men on one side, women on the other.

I think about my life and career in technology. I think about a childhood of sitting with the men, on their side of the gender barrier, followed by a career spent doing basically the same thing.

These days, more and more, I find myself sitting with the women.

I am in women-only tech startup groups on Facebook. I'm in several tech feminist Slack instances. I'm at women-in-tech conferences. I'm in broad, far-reaching Slack groups about management, but I find myself most actively contributing to the private women-only channel, tucked away in plain sight.

There is strangeness in this professional division, voluntary yet profound in its impact.

Before the Common Era

I used to have zero time for women-only, gender-split tech groups, events, or conferences.

I'm loathe to admit it now, but in my early career I wanted to be awesome—not an awesome *woman*, not awesome with boobs, just plain awesome.

Back in 2007, I attended the first She's Geeky conference. It was the first time I'd been to a women-in-tech event and I found I couldn't relate to the women there. Their situations seemed so dire, their coworkers so disrespectful, and their work environments so profoundly awful that I left feeling completely adrift.

I couldn't relate to what they were describing. I wasn't afraid to speak up in meetings. I didn't have a problem disagreeing vocally and sometimes loudly when the situation called for it.

I am naturally outspoken, I am on solid footing in tense or uncomfortable conversations, I enjoy the art of negotiation, and I have a knack for converting nervous energy into confidence. These attributes (and a bunch of privilege) helped me excel on a lopsided playing field.

At the time, nobody was talking about pipelines. We should have been paying more attention. I *wish* I'd been paying more attention. But I wasn't.

I worked with sexist asshats for years and thought the fact that I succeeded made me tough. I thought it was a commentary on my awesomeness. I ignored gender politics and got ahead.

Shanley Kane has a name for this: it's "Fuck you, I got mine" feminism. And it's problematic for a bunch of reasons she articulated back in 2013.[1]

The Common Era

Last night, I went to a dinner that was hosted blessedly close to my house. The kids wake up early, and despite not being a morning person, I'm up with them, before the sun. As a result, I'm exceptionally picky about my after-hours networking these days.

I'm at a table full of vibrant, funny, sharp ladies from a variety of fields. Some of them are also in tech (and yes, of course I already know them). But some are not.

The woman next to me leans over and says, "Okay, I'm not in tech, but I keep hearing a lot about bro culture. Is that a real thing? Have you ever had a man interrupt you or take your idea as his own or shout you down in a meeting? Does that *actually* happen?" The emphasis on *actually* indicates that it's something she's heard about but can't quite fathom. Sometimes it's the outside perspective that brings into focus how much work we still have to do.

The woman across from me is someone I adore. Like me, she's been in tech for her entire career. We make eye contact and laugh long and loud. It's the laugh of people who realize that what we find normal and commonplace is horrifying to those who don't live it every day.

We explain that what she's describing is so deeply prevalent in tech culture that it doesn't even rank as bad behavior. The worst, we explain, are things we still hesitate to say out loud because it's difficult to reconcile, even at a dinner full of successful, accomplished women, that these things happened in professional workplaces.

◆ ◆ ◆

It's such a junior move to decide you don't know how to engage with something therefore you won't engage with it at all. I didn't know how to engage with women in tech. I didn't know where my direct, naturally outspoken, comfortable with discomfort, lopsided-playing-field self fit in.

I didn't know how to talk about my day-to-day struggles alongside people who were experiencing much more horrific versions of it.

The first time I got promoted to senior management in tech, I realized just how dreadful the gender split was at senior levels. I was confronted with first-hand evidence that meritocracy is a myth that results in both a consolidated and homogeneous face of power.[2]

Over many years in tech, the ghosts from the original She's Geeky event would come back to haunt me again and again.

These were the women who should have been next to me in the boardroom. These were the women who should have been promoted alongside me. These were the women who were supposed to ride out an abusive work culture so I wouldn't have to sit with the men... alone.

I *wish* I'd been paying more attention.

I'm *trying* to pay more attention.

I hope you are too.

TWO
Growing

Everything changes as
you grow. That's true
for companies, and it's
true for people, too.

/8

How to Kill Your Startup's Referral Pipeline in a Single Interview

If you haven't checked in on your interview process in a while, do it now

> Melissa

Startups live and die by their ability to attract and retain talent. When you're just starting out, you want as many people as possible connecting you and your company with skilled folks who can help grow your business.

A busted recruiting process is a surefire way to dry up those referrals and chances are, you won't find out until it's already too late.

I'm Connected to a Bunch of Local Startups

I'm fortunate to know a bunch of amazingly talented folks. Every so often I have an opportunity to introduce a highly qualified candidate to a startup where I think the person would be a good fit.

I don't get paid for this. It's not my day job. It's just a nice thing to do that makes the universe a better place.

Occasionally people do the same thing for me when I'm hiring and looking for skilled candidates. It's not required or expected, but is lovely when it happens.

A couple of weeks ago, I find myself chatting with a friend who is thinking about her next thing, and I mention a local startup where her skills would be a great match. It doesn't mean she'll get hired, it doesn't mean she'll want to work there, but there's enough overlap that at the very least they should talk to each other.

But recruiting is like matchmaking, and sometimes, despite being a great fit on paper, people just don't hit it off.

Two Weeks Later

She writes me to say that a recruiter from the company I'd mentioned had approached her. Clearly, they had the same intuition about it being a potential fit.

I know the executive team at this startup, so I fire off a quick note to say I know the candidate and while I haven't worked with her, she's sharp and her experience might be a good fit. I get a quick thanks. And this is usually where my matchmaking stories end. Sometimes there's a fit and sometimes there isn't.

In this case, she has a successful first round, a successful second round, and a call-in for a third interview. Following the third interview, she calls me, very upset.

She Recounts What Amounts
to an Illegal Interview

The questions asked in the interview are out of bounds under both Canadian and U.S. employment law, and the interviewer was a full thirty minutes late and didn't apologize. To make matters worse, he didn't prep for the interview—didn't know who she was, hadn't seen a resumé in advance, didn't know which role she'd applied for—and it only seemed to get worse from there.

I'm livid. I debate writing a WTF email to their CEO. I debate texting their investors. I debate naming and shaming in this blog. Once I've cooled off, I realize that their worst-case scenario has already happened.

I will *never* refer another person to this company.

If asked, I would encourage people, particularly women, to interview elsewhere, as it's unlikely the interview will be fair or that the culture will be supportive of them or their careers.

People Talk

The shitty exec who asks illegal questions in an interview and hopes that no one notices is a representative of your company, your brand, and your corporate culture. Word gets around, and pretty soon you find yourself wondering why your diversity stats suck and your referral pipeline has dried up.

These are the downstream consequences of a poorly run recruiting process. They are painful, they have long-term implications on your company's ability to attract and retain top talent, and they are *entirely* preventable.

And that's the part that really hurts.

/9

Privilege, Illegal Interviews, and Burning Curiosity
An exercise in schadenfreude restraint
> Melissa

After my article about how to kill your startup referral pipeline in a single interview—this book's Chapter 8—was first published online, many members of the tech community DM'd, emailed, and slacked me to find out which startup had messed up. A couple messaged to find out which part of the interview was illegal.

Which Company?

In response to the first question, we need to talk a bit about privilege. We need to start by acknowledging that many people, particularly minorities in tech, are not in a position to write a post about every sexist or illegal hiring practice they encounter.

In my early career, I worried that speaking up about the sexism I encountered in tech would make it harder for me to get hired. Only after nearly two decades in tech am I finally at a point where I can be vocal about this stuff and not worry that it'll adversely impact my career. I don't fear that local startups will blacklist me. I don't worry that my techie friends won't want to hang out with my anymore.

It is the hallmark of privilege that I can write a post about a startup's messed-up interview process and send it out into the world, hoping I spelled everything right but not at all worried about whether it'll change the trajectory of my career.

Coming back to the original question: *Which startup are you talking about?*

Frustratingly, we're still not at a point where *minorities* can call out unfair hiring practices without concern for their careers.

The friend who had the bad interview experience is earlier in her career. She is clever and quick and eminently hirable, and some company will be incredibly lucky to have her. However, she doesn't have the privilege of giving zero fucks about pissing off hiring managers.

I do. So I wrote the post with her permission, but I'm not about to undercut her ability to get hired in the future by outing her.

Which Questions Are Illegal?

The second question that came up was from people who worried they'd been accidentally asking illegal questions in interviews. Ideally your HR teams would do interview training for first-time hiring managers, but in the event that they haven't, resources are available.[1]

The out-of-bounds questions are similar for the U.S. and Canada but there are a few notable differences. Interview rules in Europe and in Asia are *really* different, so if you're hiring globally, you'll want to check on the country-specific rules before you get started.

If you still find yourself teeming with curiosity about which company it was, I encourage you to shift that restless energy inward and focus on rooting out bad interviewing techniques within your own organization.

When I was first starting out, I learned a lot by shadowing seasoned hiring managers during the interview and offer process. I've also been fortunate to work with passionate recruiting and HR teams over the years. For more information about hiring, diversity, and inclusion, there's loads of great reading over at Model View Culture (modelviewculture.com).

/10

Your Diversity Problem Isn't the Pipeline's Fault

Stop blaming external factors, and start putting up results

> Johnathan

The results are in. They've been in for so long, so consistently, that they've become old news: diverse teams outperform.[1] Across industries and organization sizes, teams with more gender and racial diversity return stronger results to investors, retain top performers longer, and make better decisions. It's not even a close call.

And yet if your company is like any of the companies I've worked with in tech, your own diversity numbers leave a lot to be desired. When I started at Hubba, we had an all-male engineering team and four straight, white men as executives. We were nobody's model of diversity success, but it was important to us to do better. We started to get educated and to make changes like the ones described below. And we saw results. During the years I spent there, more than two-thirds of our product and engineering hires came from underrepresented groups in tech, and the benefits of a more inclusive team showed up in every aspect of our work. The team at Hubba still has a long way to go, but the critical piece they've gotten right is not to make it anyone else's fault.

Very few leaders I speak with are openly racist or sexist—most insist they'd love to build a more diverse team but ...

→ ...but they can't find quality candidates
→ ...but they post jobs and don't get minority applicants
→ ...but they don't want to lower the bar

This thinking will sink you. And your competition will run circles around you when they get to the opportunity to hire these outstanding people before you do. Here are a few of the things that we've found have generated immediate results.

Learn to Search Blindfolded

A funny thing happens when you take faces and names off of resumés and LinkedIn profiles. People who would insist that they have no bias or prejudice suddenly start evaluating candidates differently.[2] You find candidates you somehow missed before. *Unconscious bias* isn't a bleeding-heart-liberal code phrase; it's a real threat to your business and your ability to find top talent. We now use the Unbias browser add-on for Chrome to automatically hide names and faces on LinkedIn. Try it. It really does change the quality of candidate searches, whether it ought to or not.

Cast a Broader Net

A job posting has one goal: to get good candidates excited enough to start a conversation. Every time a position you post reaches some great people but they decide not to apply, your hiring program has failed. When a marketing program fails, the answer is not to complain that there aren't enough people out there; the answer is to market smarter. A job posting is no different.

Services like textio (textio.com) can help you analyze your job descriptions to find obvious points for improvement, but they're also useful for starting conversations about what you're really looking for. A long list of bullet-point requirements feels natural, but understand that those lists implicitly select for men,[3] who will apply when they meet a much smaller portion of them.

In tech, a common pattern is for hiring managers to say "I don't care who you are, just show me your hobby projects on GitHub, or your think pieces on Medium"—but a bit of reflection is all it takes to realize that screening based on free-time pursuits gets you more affluent white men than it does underemployed single moms.

Build the Best Team

The most pernicious theme I hear from people in hiring positions is that they don't want to "lower the bar"—that they'd happily hire a more diverse group but not at the cost of individual candidate quality. It sounds rational, but it's wrong-headed, for two reasons. First, the implication that any current diversity gap must be a result of lower quality stinks, and ignores everything we know about the barriers many groups face. But second is that it misunderstands your job as a leader.

Your job is to build the best team.

You can choose a lot of strategies to get there. But if your strategy is to hire "the best candidate" for each role without regard to the team's composition and it's leaving you with a weaker, less diverse team, then your strategy is failing and it needs to change.

Don't Take My Word for It

I shouldn't even be talking about this. Tech in particular has a terrible history of putting white men at the center of every conversation. But, perversely, we also know that women and minorities are frequently penalized professionally for promoting diversity.[4] Be smarter than that. There's nothing I can say that will help you nearly as much as the work that Kronda Adair, Joanne McNeil, Marco Rogers, Shanley Kane, and many others do every day. It's no one else's job to educate you on this stuff—you have to educate yourself—but there are many people who can help you on the way.

If this all seems hard, *it is*. So is building a business. Sometimes we have to do hard things. But this is the right thing to do, and the smart thing to do. Are you going to get there first, or will your competitors?

/11

The Secret to Better Interviews (and Maybe a Better Life)

It's not about what you ask them, it's about what you ask yourself

> Johnathan

Interviews suck and they don't have to. You can build an interview process that makes your candidates feel great. They will stick with you, they will feel respected, and even the ones you don't hire will refer their friends. You'll cut down on haggling at the offer stage and win against higher offers. You don't need a fifteen-person recruiting team to make it happen. You can do it yourself, and you can start today. I know this is true because I've done it.

There's only one catch.

As the employer, you have the power in an interview. To do what I'm suggesting, you have to let it go. And that starts when you think about how the other side feels.

Imbalance

As a candidate, a lot of interviews feel gross. Even when your interviewer doesn't do anything illegal (see Chapter 9), that room can feel exposed, and intimidating, and unbalanced.

The world is full of desperate advice on how to dress. How to answer questions correctly, and how much eye contact to make. What to ask, and what to *never ask*.

It sounds so unhealthy, doesn't it?

Is that how you want a candidate to think about conversations with your company? Is that how you want people to feel around you?

Some of you, if you're being honest, will say "Yes." Yes, you *do* want applicants to sweat it. To you it isn't an abuse of power. To you it's about expecting a *professional amount of preparation*. You insist that *you* went through it when *you* were coming up. You talk about *these young people today*.

And you're right, of course. It *has* been this way for a long time. But that doesn't make it right. It doesn't make it good for business, and it doesn't make it feel good, either.

If there's a theme to most of what we write here, it's that people with power need to own it. I need to own my hiring process, and you need to own yours. We don't get a pass for continuing the processes we inherited. We shouldn't want that pass. Those processes created the diversity debt and toxic culture we're all soaking in.[1] How can anyone authentically want to build a more equitable community, and be sentimental about *the good old days*?

Let Go a Little Bit

The power gap will always exist, because at some point *you* still decide whether to make an offer or not. **They** decide whether to accept—that's true. But you will meet lots of candidates and make multiple offers; they can accept only one job at a time. You face an opportunity cost and a longer search if you lose a candidate. They face rent.

Given all that, be kind. You can't flatten the power advantage you have, but you can flatten the information advantage. Use your first conversation with a candidate to talk about the process.

Who will they meet? What will those people want to talk about? What areas of the business are they responsible for, and what questions can they answer? Who should the candidate contact with questions, and what response time should they expect? How long does your process take, and where are the mile markers at which they'll know how things are going?

This gives up none of your control. You still set the timelines, process, conversation topics, and decision points. You still screen hard, still say no to candidates who don't make the cut. You don't lower the bar (see Chapter 10). All you've done so far is to tell them what's coming.

But for your candidates this is a *big change*. It's transparent. It lets them breathe, and know what to expect. The visible lift you see in people is heck of a thing. It's a tiny kernel of trust for the relationship you hope to build with them. And already it is *so different* from what they usually experience.

Let Go a Little More

Once you start to look for places where the interview process plays power games, you find them everywhere.

→ Have you noticed that job descriptions rarely *describe jobs?* They list off a vast desiderata for candidates, scaring off all but the most overconfident. To what end? What if you just explained what you were working on, what you were struggling with, and what you'd be counting on the person to do? What's the fear? That you'd have too many applicants? I've done a lot of hiring, and combing through applicants is work, for sure. But it's also a huge opportunity to spot candidates other folks missed. Weren't you complaining just last week that you'd hire more minorities if only your candidate pool was bigger?

→ Are you still using spot-test interview games like whiteboard programming exercises or surprise design quizzes? Or maybe you use "Why are manhole covers round?" or "How much water flows over Niagara Falls in a year?" They don't work.[2] They don't predict which candidates will succeed in your company. They sure *do* make candidates feel awful, though. I like practical work in the interview process, but why not make it representative? Give them some demo code with a plausible bug. Give them time to think through a fix for you two to discuss. (Give extra time, because they have a life outside of your process.) If you need it to be in person, pair-program something or review an API together.

→ Don't make your candidates ask about maternity benefits or paternal leave policies. It's easy to see why that's a terrifying thing for a candidate to ask. I promise that if you mention it to every single candidate, some of them won't care and the rest will really, really appreciate it (see Chapter 34).

→ Invite them to help set the interview schedule. Who do they need to meet to understand the gig? I've rarely had people take me up on it, but twice I know that invitation was the difference between us getting the hire or not.

If these aren't your things, pick different ones. Get creative. You could talk about salary up front to get rid of all *that* awful power imbalance. Or you could provide references to candidates instead of the other way around. You could offer to schedule interviews well outside of business hours for people who can't get the time off, or open your company's childcare services up to candidates.

I can't tell you which changes make sense for you, but I know that the exercise itself has value. When you spend the time to understand what's terrifying about your interview process, you are better for it.

And You Will Still Screw Up

Trying to clean up the power games in the process won't save you from mistakes. Until you put processes in place to catch it, you'll still sometimes fail to follow up. I know I've done it. I feel crappy about it, and I use systems now to try to prevent it, but I'm sure that doesn't make the candidate feel any better.

You'll still have candidates who feel like they didn't get a fair shot. You'll still have bias throughout that you'll need to push hard against. I'm not selling magic beans here.

But you will have done a humane thing for the world just the same. Your employees will come into your organization with a different sense of identity and a different set of expectations. *The place will feel different.* And remember, these power discrepancies always hit the people on the margins hardest. If you work at it, you might find that equalizing the power a little also helps improve the diversity of your team. Candidates who would have dropped out stick through and feel welcomed.

At least that's the hope. And anyhow, what do you have to lose?

/12

You Can't Be What You Can't See

Why visible diversity in tech matters

> Melissa

The first time I heard this phrase—*You can't be what you can't see*—it was about diversity in jobs. I can't recall whether it was specifically about women in tech or people of color in leadership or all of the above, but the phrase stuck with me. And every so often, my brain takes it back out and plays with it.

Recently the *New York Times* ran a piece about tech belt-tightening. It quoted or profiled eight people. All of them were men; the majority of them were white. I read the piece wondering how a reporter came to interview all men for a tech piece and didn't notice (?), didn't care (?), or, worse, didn't think speaking to female tech execs or entrepreneurs would provide an important perspective for the piece (?!).

And then I think about that reporter's editor who didn't notice, didn't care, or didn't think there was anything missing or wrong about the story as it was eventually published. Never mind that female execs are routinely championed for running tighter financial ships than their male counterparts. Never mind that it was 20 fucking 16. Never mind that it's the *New York* fucking *Times*. Never mind any of that.

I think about PC culture. I think about the Benetton ads from the '80s. I think about my biracial nephew and how many families look like his. I think about his mom, who still struggles to find him a doll that looks like him.

I think about the evolution of stock photography. I think about the many startups that show exclusively white hands in all of their product shots because it doesn't occur to them that this excludes a large swath of humanity.

You can't be what you can't see.

I think about growing up in Baltimore where the majority is a minority. Growing up, all the Barbies on TV had brown skin, all the newscasters had brown skin, almost all the people I saw in commercials had brown skin. I'm in college the first time I see a Burger King commercial with a white person in it. It comes crashing down on me in one cynical wave that Baltimore has demographic-specific advertising and that it's different from the advertising in other places.

Earlier this week, I watched a startup launch with a website hastily thrown together before the announcement. I scroll through the site. There isn't a single woman on it. The people who put together the site didn't notice (?), didn't care (?), or didn't know any women who they thought worthy of putting on the website (?).

Except...I know the people who put it together.

I want them to be bros. I want them to be idiots. I want them to be the worst versions of white men in tech. But they're not. They're dads, of little girls. They speak loudly and publicly about the need for greater diversity in tech. They know it's a problem, and they care about fixing it.

I scroll farther down the page. There are stick figures. The stick figures are all men.

You can't be what you can't see.

I can't see a single woman on a page showcasing innovation and entrepreneurship in tech. It's not that I don't know women who fit that description, it's that I can't *see* them.

I can't see a single woman in a *New York Times* piece about responsible stewardship during a downturn.

I go through a week of this, of flagging for people that they missed a step and that, whether or not it's on purpose, it's a problem. And it's the little problem of all male stick figures and how that factors into the bigger problem of making tech a big enough tent so everyone's contributions can be recognized and valued.

I'm exhausted. I'm tired of being grumpy. I'm tired of having to spot it, see it, and then teach other people about something they would have seen first if they'd only *noticed, cared,* or *thought about the implications of making women or people of color invisible.*

You can't be what you can't see.

/13

Big Lies, Little Lies, and the Cheat Code to a Promotion

And also a tiny cheerleader, in case that's all you need

> Johnathan

I talk with a lot of people about their careers. Maybe you're one of them. Sometimes you work for a team that I run, but more often you don't. You've been introduced to me one way or another, probably by someone I trust, so I try to be helpful.

The majority of the time, people who say they want to talk about their career really want *permission*. Permission to quit their job. Permission to change the direction of their career, or the way they tell their story. They know that things aren't working for them, and they have a vision of what "better" feels like.

I don't have any permission over their lives to give, but I try to listen. I validate where I can. I challenge where I feel like I should.

Mostly, those people need me to be their tiny cheerleader.

Is this is you? When you're thinking about a change like this, it helps to know that other people are in your corner. I can't give you permission, but I *can* agree with your analysis and support you. If this is you, you don't need to read the rest of this chapter.

I believe in you. You can do the thing. *Go you!*

The Other Conversation

The other way those conversations go is that you don't want to move *out*, you want to move *up*. Usually this conversation happens when you're pretty early in your career, but not always. I've had this conversation with people older than me, too.

I wish someone had had it with me earlier in my own career.

It often starts with frustration. You deserve a promotion you're not getting. You're due. Or maybe it's not *quite* that you're due, it's that you don't really know how to get there. You're confused as much as anything. Everyone seems to be playing the same game but no one will tell you the rules.

This can be true even if your company isn't totally broken. Having a good manager and clear role definitions help, sure. But humans are funny people. We make a lot of our decisions without really knowing why.[1] Your manager, especially if they're new, might not actually be able to articulate this stuff either.

So you hunt. You read terrible Medium posts. You get advice from your family and friends in other fields. And yet here we find ourselves, with you frustrated and me taking a breath and saying,

That's unlikely to work out the way you want it to.

Here's where the conversation goes next.

The Big Lie: Time in Role or Time at Company Leads to Growth

A lot of people I meet who haven't managed before think seniority, or time in role, is a big part of the promotion calculation. It makes sense from their perspective. They've invested a lot of time and energy in the company, and they deserve recognition for that investment.

It's a lie. And worse: some shops reinforce that lie. During my time at IBM, for example, it was very hard for managers to promote someone who hadn't been in their current role for at least two or three years. I've even seen some particularly weak managers make this choice deliberately. They use the fact that someone's stuck around for three or four years as the *main* argument for a promotion. I have never seen that scenario end well.

Generally, this is a dangerous lie to believe, because it violates the cardinal rule of promotions. A promotion should happen when the organization has (1) a need for a more senior role and (2) confidence that the employee will succeed in it. This rule doesn't say anything about "or when the employee has hung around long enough" because promotions are not participation ribbons.

Promotions bring new responsibilities and scope, and more authority over the work of others. They should happen with thought and consideration, not as a default outcome. And if you *do* get in through sheer longevity, I doubt very much that the new role will fulfill or stretch you.

Even in teams where this *is* a realistic path to climbing, it's the slowest, crappiest path around. You might linger long enough to pick up a new title, but the opportunity costs you pay for this approach are immense. If you can afford to, my advice is to *get out*. Don't waste another five years on hold for the next round.

The Little Lie: Keep Your Head Down and Crank Out Work

As a baseline strategy, this sucks less. When you're early in your career or junior within your current function, working hard on whatever comes your way is a good start. Even with bad managers and unclear roles, the opportunity to practice your craft is helpful.

The problem with this approach was nicely illustrated by Satya Nadella, the CEO of Microsoft. When asked what women seeking advancement should do, he gave some awful (and quickly retracted) advice:[2] he suggested that women should work hard and wait for karma to catch up. I want it to work that way, but it doesn't. Hard work *is* correlated with success, but the system sure does value some people's hard work over others'.

By all means, work hard. Deep skill in a few functional areas gives you a foundation you can build a rich and rewarding career on. And attentive managers *do* sometimes say, "We need to give Kim a bigger role—she's tearing through the stuff we put in front of her." But unless you're coming from a privileged place to begin with, hard work alone is rarely enough.

The Cheat Code: Understand the Business

I wish there was a way, Matrix-style, to upload this next bit into people's brains. I haven't found the words to do it yet, though I'll try again here. I hope you'll tell me if it connects.

The #1 best predictor I've seen for a person's future career success is that they understand the business they're in.

Understand the business. Not your team's goals, the business as a whole. Develop a genuine curiosity about how it all works, and keep going until you get it. Ask executives and people in other teams. Look up your competitors and go through their sign-up flows. Talk to customers if you can, or at least to the people who do. Do Google searches for the stuff your team does and see who owns the Adwords and the top 10 hits. Don't tune out during all-hands meetings. If you're at a startup, ask to see pitch decks. If you're a public megacorp, dial in to earnings calls.

This cheat code often works for a few different reasons:

→ **Visibility.** You can't understand a business from within a single department. In order to get your head around it, you'll inevitably talk to people from all over. In addition to context, this develops a network of colleagues who believe that you *get* them and value their work. This cycle feeds on itself, as those people are likely to give you more context as they learn new things.

→ **Relevance.** The problem with junior people is rarely that they lack energy and ideas. It's that their ideas are often shallow or misaligned with the company strategy. As you understand the business and context around your work, your questions and ideas start to cut to the important bits. You won't take distracting goals. You'll be drawn toward the critical path. The stuff you're excited to work on will be the stuff with the highest business impact. This doesn't work every time, but it's a pattern I've seen repeat.

→ **Self-direction.** As you get more senior, the onus for future advancement falls less and less on your manager and more and more on you. When you understand the direction of the business, you're able to identify gaps. Your plan to address those gaps is probably the best one anyone's heard. Assuming you've identified a problem that matters, you're in a better position than most to get asked to tackle it.

While the other folks in your org *can* do these things, most people won't. The result is that you have the opportunity for outsized impact. When your manager makes the case for a promotion, you're more likely to have a chorus of support from other teams. That helps.

Playing on Hard Mode

None of this is a guarantee. All other things being equal, it works better than other strategies I've seen, *but all other things aren't equal.* Like every other career strategy in tech, this stuff works much better if you're white and male. And that's shitty, because most of you aren't.

It would be stupid for me to pretend that I know what that feels like…To get patronizing answers to smart questions because your English is accented. To be a woman told to be less "outspoken" and "shrill" when no man would get that feedback.[3] I haven't lived that, and I don't have any quick cheat codes for you to unbreak that busted-ass system.

But I know there are managers reading this, too, and you folks *can* change it. Check yourselves. Learn how bias messes with the way you hear your team and recognize their growth. Figure out how much privilege helped get you where you are. Engage with the syllabus.[4] Every day you have people in your company who are either going to move up or move out and you're burning them with this ignorance. Be better. That's the job.

No Path But What You Make

This might not be your path. And moving up might not be your aim. There are infinite ways to move forward or sideways that might fit you better. My main goal here is to keep you away from the lies, not steer you toward a solitary truth. But whatever your path, my hope is that you find your way to impact, not just longevity.

And if it helps at all: I believe in you. You can do the thing.

/14

Obvious to You Is Not the Same as Obvious

Being oblivious to what is and
is not obvious

> Melissa

"What's the biggest lesson you learned in the past year? Business lesson, I mean," I am asked.

I know it immediately, and I wish I could say it's a new lesson, one I haven't had to learn over and over again. But it's not. This one comes out of my mouth before I can even process the fact that it's one I first learned about ten years ago.

I'm 26

I'm sitting on the floor of the CEO's office. This happens a lot in the old days of Mozilla. We're in Building K. We're still in the offices across the street from the Googleplex on Shoreline.

I'm running PR, and while my skills are solid, I'm young. There's a bunch of stuff I still have to learn, and much of it will come through real-world experience.

John Lilly is Mozilla's CEO. He asks about our recent media coverage and I rattle off a few observations. Nothing formal, just some off-the-cuff stuff that I've noticed.

John jumps on it—"Why haven't you shared that internally?"

I stop, think about it, and respond:

"Because everyone has access to the same Google alerts. I'm not seeing anything they aren't getting in their inbox. And I'm not noticing anything any other rational human wouldn't see when faced with the same information."

Oh boy.

I'm 36

It's been ten years since I sat on the floor in a Mountain View office park and unlocked one of the greatest secrets in my professional life.

Obvious to you is not the same as obvious.

I'm sitting at my desk and I overhear a colleague talking. "Well, for anyone who uses the product, it's obvious."

I peek over my monitor. "I use the product. What's obvious?"

She goes on to share an interesting insight about our users. I follow up: "That's awesome and interesting and *not at all obvious.* I use the product, but I don't use it in the way that you're describing. And even if I did, it's unlikely I'd see the same thing. It's obvious to you because you're immersed in this stuff. How lucky for us that you are!"

Lucky You, Lucky Us

Lucky you. You get to do a job where you bring your natural ability to work. You pay attention. You notice patterns. You spot trends.

You can rattle off the top 5 ways our users are hacking our platform right now. When faced with the same information as everyone else, you see things that matter to the business.

Lucky us. We employ you. We benefit from you thinking about one area of our business in depth, be it product, marketing, design, recruiting, or something else entirely. We reap the reward of you having all the context that comes with sitting in your seat. But we don't get any of the value of you having that full-time vantage point **unless you share what you see.**

Without finding it's way out into the business, the profound insight you've had is the same as the profound insight you haven't had. It has no bearing on our day-to-day operations.

Ten Years In

I no longer find it surprising that, faced with the same access to the same information, several reasonably clever people draw radically different conclusions.

My friend Mike says it's okay to fail; you just shouldn't keep failing in the same way over and over again.

Ten years in, I'm still learning and relearning this lesson. To be fair, I'm learning different versions of it. Perhaps that means I still pass Mike's test.

These days, the version I work on is about how to contextualize my decisions so my staff know these are more than mercurial whims.

We sit in different meetings. We have different conversations.

My job requires that I'm in touch with the business strategy—not as some far-off nebulous thing to be revisited on a quarterly or annual basis, but as the driving undercurrent that informs all my interactions.

This means I'm often representing a unique perspective in conversations. Things that are obvious to me, with one foot in strategy and one foot in operations, aren't obvious to many other executives, even though they are also splitting their time between these worlds.

On a near daily basis, I'm reminded that this ability to see what others cannot is a gift. The things I can see that they cannot are not better or worse than the things they can see that I cannot.

I nudge myself to share, especially the things that seem obvious. This is usually an indication that I've thought about them long and hard.

When the reasons seem evident, I try to dig in on the why. I try to show my work, to go back and turn my slow hunches into useful, meaningful business intelligence.

And I push the people around me to do the same. Because I know that the things they can see that others cannot are *their* gift.

It's not better or worse.

It's not obvious.

It's just different.

/15

How to Negotiate
Like a Boss
3 salary negotiation mistakes you're
probably making right now
> Melissa

Last week, a friend pinged about an upcoming salary negotiation. In advance of the discussion, she's talking to lots of folks so she can learn from all our mistakes. I *wish* I'd been clever enough to ask for this type of advice in my twenties.

As I talk about how my approach to salary negotiations has evolved since my twenties, I'm *mortified*. So many of the things I thought were fixed or non-negotiable turned out to be the opposite. And so much of what freaked me out turned out to be no big deal.

And here's the terrifying part: **The thing I thought was no big deal was the biggest fuck-up of all.** A perpetuating-inequality-and-wage-gap type fuck-up. We'll get there.

But first, let's check in on twenty-something me and see how she's doing...

Mistake #1: The Quiet Wait. The Budding Resentment.

Early in my career, I dreaded asking for a raise. I figured it was easier to do great work, keep my head down, and hope that someone noticed.

In 2014, the CEO of Microsoft, Satya Nadella, went to the Grace Hopper Conference and *told women in tech not to ask for raises*. He basically quoted twenty-two-year-old me. And twenty-two-year-old me was an idiot.

Keep your head down. Work hard. Hope someone notices. I developed that approach in 2002. It was wrong then; it was still wrong in 2014. Satya's mea culpa tweet quickly followed his onstage comments.

This approach is busted for so many reasons. To stand up as the CEO of a major tech company in 2014 and deliver this advice on stage at the GHC ... Pretty sure *gobsmacked* is the word I'm looking for.

For startups that are notoriously crappy at both mythical meritocracy and HR as a function, this advice is a recipe for disaster. In this environment, if you fail to get a raise or get ahead, you don't know if it's because you didn't work hard enough or if it's because of the irregular and unstructured performance reviews. Or the woefully vague and unactionable feedback. Or compensation reviews that don't adhere to a schedule.

Without a clear sense of the process, people spend a bunch of time wondering when, exactly, is the right time to bring up their salary.

TO DO: Schedule the awkwardness

Set a time to meet to talk about compensation. And at the end of that discussion, set up the next discussion (typically six to twelve months in the future). And then go put a reminder on your calendar. That way you don't have to worry that you're pestering or nagging or otherwise annoying anyone. You're simply following up.[1] The same way you always do. Because you're amazing.

Mistake #2: Everything Has Changed...
Except for Your Salary

My murky startup job meant that I got to take on a bunch of new responsibilities. My role then changed from individual contributor (IC) to manager. I went from being U.S.-focused to covering a global business. I completed major projects, on time, and with awesome outcomes.

But despite big changes in my roles and responsibilities, my salary stayed the same. I would get a knot in my stomach every time I thought about approaching my boss. *Ugh—maybe I'll just wait until the end of next quarter.*

Inevitably, another quarter would come and go without any movement. I would swear to myself I'd bring it up next time...and then chicken out.

This cycle continued for years.

I started to lead bigger teams and hire more people. That process taught me a ton about how people negotiate, what the HR folks have in mind, and how salaries are set. With that knowledge, it was no longer this opaque, terrifying process. It was actually pretty straightforward.

I had always felt super weird about *asking for a raise*. The *asking* part felt odd—as though the raise were an allowance or my parent's car keys on a Saturday night. And the *raise* part felt weird—what if they say yes but we have different amounts in mind?

And then I learned the most amazing phrase. Ready?

✧ COMPENSATION REVIEW ✧

(or *comp review* or *comp assessment* or *salary review*).

Let's hold these gems up side by side and see if we can spot the difference:

→ **"Asking for a Raise"**: *Please* let me have jumped through the right hoops at the right moments. *Please* let this be the perfect day, when my boss is in a good mood, the sun is shining, and I have had stellar performance on a recent project.

→ **"Compensation Review"**: Well, *hello* there, formalized HR approach! Your salaries are set by the market and assessed every so often to make sure to pay similar rates for similar roles at similar companies? Where you been all my life?

Once I figured out that comp reviews were pretty commonplace for grown-up organizations, the whole mess of salary negotiation got a lot easier.

Here are some other handy ways to indicate that you think you might be underpaid without having to *say* that you think you are underpaid (or an offer is too low):

→ **"I want to make sure my comp is in step with market rates for this role."** This is useful if you have a well-defined role (designer, engineer, sales associate) and are in a location where many people do that same job. San Francisco has zillions of senior engineers. Their salaries may vary, but you can at least get a sense of market rate by doing some online research (try starting at salary.com).

→ **"My responsibilities have changed and I'm excited about this new and challenging role. I'd love to set up a time to update my job spec, make sure we've got the same things in mind, and conduct a comp review."** Early-stage startups will struggle with this. They may not have job descriptions. They may not know what a comp review is. But unless they are a super tiny shop, chances are good there was a job posting that they used when they hired you. If you take a look and everything is different, it's time for a chat to get back on the same page.

→ **"Can you share the salary band or range for this position and how you anticipate an employee will progress through the band?"** Basically what you're asking for here is for them to tell you the high and low end of salary for the role. Then you want to know how they think about the job criteria at the low, middle, and high points of that salary.

TO DO: Check in on the market

If you got hired in 2010 and haven't had a raise since, chances are good you're well out of sync with market rates. Market rates don't usually swing too wildly. But for emerging technologies (AI, big data, VR), what was once a nascent skill set may suddenly be in very high demand. Check in on the market yearly.

Find mentors in your network, people you feel comfortable asking for advice. Senior folks have usually hired for every stage of your career. They can give you a rough idea of what to expect along the way.

Many venture capital firms have people on staff to help portfolio companies set salaries for various stages of investment (from seed on up). Find one of those people and buy them a coffee.

Mistake #3: The Biggest Fuck-up of All

For the bosses reading this, I need you to take a moment. Imagine the spreadsheet that HR sends out, the one with the hidden columns. The one that lists the salaries of everyone on your team and their start dates and the last time they got a raise.

Now imagine you're in the middle of a bunch of tasks. In addition to your usual fifty open tabs, you have a bunch of open emails. You are trying to respond to HR with the updated salary data, but instead of sending it to your internal contact, *you accidentally send it to the entire editorial team at the New York Times*. They print the spreadsheet on the front page of the next day's newspaper.

How do you feel? Are you okay with what your staff will see in the news? Or do you cringe? Are you panicked about that glaring disparity between employees who are doing the same job with the same level of experience, the one you've been meaning to fix but haven't?

Oops.

You may not ever have your salary data show up in the *New York Times*, but it's a useful test for how you're doing. You should assume that people talk, that after spending day in and day out with their colleagues, people will get comfortable. And at some point that conversation may turn to discussions about salary. That's okay. They aren't doing anything wrong. It's their personal information, and they're allowed to share it as they wish.

Your job is not to prevent those discussions. Your job is to make sure that when those discussions happen, everything passes the sniff test.

TO DO: Take the time to make it right

You inherited the team. You didn't hire them into those weird salary ranges—they were like that when you got there. It's not your fault, as such.

But if you've managed that crew for more than a month without a plan to address it, you're complicit. Your inaction has perpetuated a salary structure that isn't defensible. It's going to be a giant pain in the ass to fix it. It will require input from HR and senior management, and a bunch of your time to chase down the details. But it's your job. And you will sleep better at night for knowing you pass the *New York Times* test.*

One Last Thing: Samba Not Combat

Here's the secret truth about salary negotiation that anyone who's done a bunch of it can tell you: At the end of the negotiation, you still have to work together.

If you are the hiring manager and your inbound employee feels totally screwed, that's a terrible way to start things off. And if you are trying to close a candidate with unrealistic salary expectations who won't budge, that also sucks.

In the best circumstances, salary negotiation is a dance, not a fight. It's a back and forth—a step forward, a step back, one to the

---

* The amazing part about this test is that *the actual New York Times did not pass this test.*[2]

right or left. And, finally, a decision to go forward together... or to part ways.

Conversations about money are uncomfortable. Even when negotiations aren't about money, they're uncomfortable. Depending on your upbringing, background, and relative privilege in the world, that discomfort can range from mild to paralyzing. Everything in this post is something I wish I'd known at some stage in my career, but if you'd told me some of this in my twenties, I probably wouldn't have known what to do with it.

And that's not only because twenty-two-year-old me was an idiot. It took me a while to find my voice, to feel confident, and to have the awkward conversations along the way. And even after all that, I still had to get over my imposter syndrome to finally get paid what I was worth.

Wherever you are in that cycle, I hope this helps.

/16

You Know Your Product Team Is Failing. Do You Know Why?

Would you believe me if I told you that it's almost always the same, fixable thing?

> Johnathan

I build teams that build products. It's my thing that I do—engineering, design, marketing, and product management. That's what I did with the pretty big Firefox team at Mozilla. That's what I did as a consultant with tiny to medium-sized startups in Toronto. That's what I'm doing now with the growing and amazing team at Hubba. I love it.

Are you in charge of a startup product team? Do you love it? Because, and I want to be honest here, a lot of the people I talk to who run product groups are not having a good time. They're not even having an *okay* time.

They are having a *not okay* time.

What It Feels Like

The hard thing about a busted product org is that the problem isn't obvious. The engineers seem to know what they're doing. The product managers have roadmaps. The designers are always busy and things look nice. But it *just. doesn't. work.*

Your team seems to run fast, they ship a lot of code, but features take forever. You never feel like you know when something's going to come out. When it does, it never looks like you thought it would. The engineers celebrate when they complete a heavy project, but the rest of the org doesn't get why it ever mattered. People don't respond to new features, and bugs in old features never get attention. Things break that we should have seen coming and you have to drop everything to fix them ... which makes the other problems worse.

If you're hyperventilating right now, I feel you. I've been where you are. I wrote this chapter for *us*.

Whose Fault Is It

"Everyone's fault. No one's fault." I think I'm supposed to say those things. That there are a hundred reasons for product teams to fail to execute well. I guess that's probably true.

But in my own life, almost every team I've seen struggle with this stuff fails for the same reason. There is one role in the product organization that we ask to be the integrators, the systematizers. And companies, especially startups, usually set them up to fail. We call those people Product Managers.

If your product managers aren't on their game and well supported, you will have a bad time. *Not because it's always their fault*, at all, but because when they're in trouble, strength in other areas is unlikely to compensate.

How to Build Your Product Team

Any time I write a new job posting for a product manager, I brace for impact. Few people would apply to be heart surgeons or forensic accountants without any relevant experience. But *lots* of people apply to be product managers without experience. *Everyone* thinks they'd be good at product.

If none of your founders or executives have run product orgs before, it can be hard to know what to do with these candidates. They have so many *amazing ideas*. They have a lot of *energy*.

If you find yourself saying something like "Anyone can learn how to file bugs and run a standup, but what I like about this person is ...," you're about to make a mistake.

Hire product managers as product managers

There are lots of times in the growth of a startup when you should take a gamble on candidates with gumption even if they don't have the background. It's a great strategy for building a more diverse team, and it gives your senior folks mentorship opportunities. There are many times when it's a wise and progressive call to make.

But your first few product management hires *are not one of those times*. Your first PMs will set the tone for how your product team operates. And since few people have any kind of formal education in product management, your best indicator is significant, direct product management experience.

After those first few hires are in and operating well, go ahead and hire some trainees. Build a reputation for product excellence by training people up and setting the standard. Your people may get poached, but your inbound candidate pool will more than cover it.

That's a high-quality place to be, but not until you've locked on fundamentals.

Hire product managers not visionaries

Oh, I know, it's unromantic. Great product needs vision. And good CEOs want partners in setting that vision. You want PMs who understand it and can bring their own light to it. I've heard all that, and it's not wrong.

But the truth is that I need vision from my PMs about 5 to 10% of the time. I need brilliant, focused, measured execution from them *all* the time.

I didn't say 0% vision—don't straw-man me. Vision matters.

But ideas are cheap and execution is very, very hard.

Interview for the hard part. Hire for the hard part.

Product management is a real discipline, not a pretend catch-all title. That "anyone can learn" garbage up there undercuts the value of clear requirements, clean process, measurement, and accountability. Your product managers put the machine on rails and make sure it gets to its destination.

Vision is one of the tools they use to get there. The whole team benefits from clarity in the product's narrative. You'll meet candidates who blow you away with their list of ideas, who've prepared over the weekend by looking at your product. It's exciting.

But if they can't tell you when a waterfall development process would be a better choice than scrum, or how they feel about personas as a user-empathy tool, or how they prefer to see new features instrumented, they aren't your first product hire. Or at least, they wouldn't be mine.

Hire product managers not CEOs of the product

Poor Ben Horowitz. He said, "The product manager is the CEO of the product" and I suspect he's regretted it ever since.[1] His intention was noble enough—arguing for buck-stop accountability and whole-product view. But it has armed a generation of asshats with a terrible self-importance. He even wraps that post with a disclaimer these days.

Your product managers are not the CEO of anything. They can't fire people who are hurting the business. They can't sign partnership deals. They do not live the five hundred daily struggles of trying to keep everything alive and growing. It's facile to pretend that the analogy holds.

PMS are much more hub-of-the-wheel than root-of-the-tree or top-of-the-pyramid. They synthesize, they decide, and they orchestrate. As Andy Grove would say: Input, Process, Output.[2] If you think of them as a CEO, you'll manage the good ones badly and keep the bad ones around too long.

Be curious about how they listen and seek counterpoint during the synthesis phase. Challenge them on how they make trade-offs in the deciding and planning phase. Measure them based on their results in the orchestration and delivery phase.

How to Know It's Working

When you've got good product leadership, the chaos starts to make sense. You ship fewer features, but they speak directly to customer needs. They come with instrumentation so that you can measure their impact. Great ideas get amplified; missed attempts are spotted and quickly culled.

When your product team is working, the product connects directly to the strategy of the business. You can see how the roadmap elements move the needles you care about. You can elevate the conversation from "Ship this feature by Friday" to "How should we tailor our onboarding to maximize engagement for different kinds of users?" Your PMS start to surprise you with vision and creativity rooted in reality. What they do makes sense. It matters.

This rarely happens right away. In my experience, good PMS often start with the safe, obvious bits. It helps them get processes in place and ensures that they put up some immediate wins to earn the respect of their engineers and the broader team. On that foundation, I expect to see them take broader autonomy and scope pretty quickly and make the product their own.

A product manager who's still running someone else's road map a year in is effectively a *project* manager. A product manager that throws the road map away on Day 1 in favor of their new vision is very likely a liability.

What If It's Too Late?

You've already hired them, haven't you. The ideas people. The CEOs of the product. And maybe you're reading this and it makes some sense to you but you don't think your existing team can get there.

You might be right.

But let's choose to believe in them. Most people can learn most things. And I'm a really big fan of treating people like adults. So talk with them about this stuff. Ask them what they think of it, and what supports they need. Ask them if they agree.

And they might not. It might be that they are not going to work out in your organization. But that can be okay.

If your team does agree that they need a change, they'll still need support to make it real. And so my second piece of advice, worth whatever you paid for it, is to hire an experienced product leader to drive that cultural shift.

Most product leaders *love* building things, and this is a good meaty role for the right candidate. Give them the founder's vision. Expect them to want to see pitch decks and understand the state of the business. Get them to meet your existing product folks to see the potential that's waiting to be unlocked. You can do it.

Sorry Not Sorry

If any of this stuck, I've made your job harder. You had such a huge candidate pool before! You could hire *exciting people* with *great ideas!* Now you have to hunt, and you need your prey to have well-developed operational chops. There are fewer of those people, and they are more hotly contested for by savvy organizations that know what they're trying to build.

But I'm not sorry. The people you need are out there. They work hard, they rarely get the credit, and they deserve to be courted. It can be thankless to wrangle a team of engineers and designers week after week, particularly when the output is "reliable, measured, upward progress," which is easy to take for granted. So if I drive up their market rate a bit, I'm not sorry at all.

Go find them. Add your vision to theirs and their system to yours. Make something amazing.

/17

Valley Extraction: How to Hire Senior Talent Away from Silicon Valley in Four Easy Steps

Catch your own unicorn hire!

> Melissa

In 2001, I moved to San Francisco. I didn't have a job lined up. I had a sublet for two months. I figured if I got a job, I'd stay, and if I didn't, I'd move back east and get a job closer to family. This was in the midst of tech's nuclear winter, the age of pink-slip parties and mass layoffs. It was an utterly ridiculous time to pick up and move to SF on a whim, but, like so many other great San Francisco adventures, practicality had nothing to do with it.

I got a job offer on week 7 of my two-month sublet. And so began my SF tech story. Thirteen years later, I fell in love with a Canadian and relocated to Toronto, thus closing out an amazing stretch of my professional life spent bopping between 101, 280, and SoMa.

One of the things that strikes me often is how ungettable people think Valley talent is. A colleague is hiring for her team and I asked if she wanted me to ping some friends in California to see if they were interested or would help connect her to people who might be right for the role. She felt like the odds of finding someone and then having them want to move were slim.

But there's nothing magical about California people. Some of them are awesome, some of them are not. There are mediocre people at Google. There are slackers at Facebook. Those are not the people we're talking about. We're talking about the people who have been in the trenches, learned a bunch of stuff along the way, and are ready to apply that knowledge in a different context.

From someone who's lived in SF and worked in the Bay Area for a decade plus, here are four steps to loosen the Silicon Valley death grip on talent you'd like to recruit.

1. Be the good kind of creepy

The good news is that most Valley tech talent has a healthy online presence. Are they on Twitter? Facebook? LinkedIn? Instagram? What, it's all of the above? Even better.

Learn what you can. Are they originally from somewhere else? Do they have family near where your company is headquartered? Perhaps they are looking for a reason to move back. Are they dating a Canadian? If so, they might find themselves more open to winter than they previously thought possible.

Are they about to become parents for the first time? Do they have kids who are about to start school? These are key moments. These are "take stock of life, look around, and decide if you're really happy" moments. And people who have otherwise enjoyed the shiny futuristic awesome that is Silicon Valley may not want to raise their kids there.

California's already limited housing supply becomes even more overwrought in high-quality school districts. Particularly for people who want to live in the city not the surrounding 'burbs, schooling is a major concern. Private-school tuition for multiple children is not viable for a lot of people.

I sat out the nuclear winter by crunching and analyzing data about how families were being displaced in San Francisco. This was fifteen years ago. The situation has only gotten worse. Many people are looking for a place where they can raise a family and not have both parents working crazy-long weeks just to cover the basics.

2. Ask for advice

Silicon Valley people love a good challenge. When Wattpad CEO Allen Lau was coming out to SF for TechCrunch Disrupt a few years ago, he asked if I'd meet him for coffee. We'd never met before, but a friend was working at Wattpad and suggested he and I get together to talk about marketing and PR for consumer tech companies. We had a great meeting and at the end he said, "Now I just need to find someone like you but in Toronto." We laughed.

At the time, I wasn't considering a move, but when it became clear that I was going to resettle my life in Toronto, guess who was one of my first calls?

It's a good recruiting trick to ask people for advice. Getting them thinking about your business, the space you play in, the problems you're trying to solve, the challenges, opportunities, etc.—these are all great ways to get them excited about your company. And while they may not be ready to make a move immediately,

and might not ever, your worst-case scenario is that you got a
smart person thinking about your business.

3. Don't compete on perks

You will lose. The Valley
will out-perk you.
They will out-snack you.
They will out-beer you.
They will out-foosball you.
They will out-beanbag-
chairs-jauntily-strewn-
about-the-office you.
You will lose.

And that's okay.

You will win on things people who have been over-perked care
about. You will win on work–life balance. You will win on commute

time. You will win on livability and affordability and housing prices and taxes (not you, Canada). Just ask Austin, Texas.

There are may ways to score a job opportunity. Perks are commodities. Yes, they're nice, and yes, it's a neat way to impress your friends and family who have to pay for coffee at work. But if we're honest about it, the in-house barista is a bit extravagant, a bit silly, and he always overroasts the espresso.

Move the field. Offer perks that the Valley can't, like a strong social safety net, a robust universal health care system, and a shockingly functional public school system (there you go, Canada).

4. Play the long game

You may not get your unicorn hire. They may never want to leave catered meals, free oil changes, or Flowbee haircuts in a trailer on campus (the Flowbee part is made up; the haircuts are real). But if you can close those unicorns, there are real benefits to bringing senior Valley tech talent to your town.

Assuming they're great, they will not only help level up your team, they will also contribute to building out a robust local ecosystem. They will mentor, coach, and support growing businesses. They will spot trends and avoid missteps because they've seen scale at work.

And they will tell their friends how great it is to work there, how short the commute is, how cheap the rent is, how great the schools are, how neat it is to have seasons, and how they can't imagine living anywhere else.

And that's the best free advertising for capturing your next unicorn hire.

/18

Why More Companies Don't Do Remote Work (and Probably Shouldn't)

Hint: It's not actually that they hate freedom

> Johnathan

The sun never set on the Firefox empire. In my years at Mozilla, one of our secret weapons was our global community of volunteers and employees. It allowed us to release Firefox in 80+ languages at once. It meant we could hire the best people wherever they were in the world and not have to end every job description with the tired old

Must be willing to relocate to San Francisco.

When it worked, it worked really well. We had lively 24/7 newsgroups, IRC, and bug chatter. We were early adopters of multi-way videoconferencing rigs. We alpha-tested telepresence robots. We wikied our meeting notes. We made heavy use of the world clock meeting planner at timeanddate.com. Our systems forced us to write down decisions and maintain single sources of truth because the default assumption was that our colleagues weren't local.

As an individual member of the team, I think it looked like it mostly worked, most of the time. I bet the me of 2007, giddy with what our community was capable of, would have agreed with the universal *rightness* of remote work.

Yes, well...

Hindsight Is a Hell of a Thing

I should say, before elaborating on what changed my mind, that this is a pretty uncomfortable spot to be in. The rightness of remote work is a given for many tech folk. As a community, we put a high premium on nomadism. Asking people to show up all together in a physical office feels campy and outdated, like asking them to work regular 9-to-5 office hours or to dress in business suits. It's a dusty, old-person thing to want. It makes me sound *ancient*.

What's worse, someone who attacks remote work is implicitly engaging in all kinds of privilege enforcement. Compared to working in an SF (or NY, or Toronto) office, remote work is cheaper, more flexible, and more accessible to people with disabilities that make commuting a challenge. When you demand in-office work, you give advantage to people with wealth, mobility, and a lack of outside commitments. Why on earth would you make the decision to do those things?

It's obvious: You're either pro-remote or you're a monster.

I Am Not a Monster

There are three reasons—no, three *categories* of reasons—why I no longer see things that way. I want to be clear, though, so clear that I just *bet* I'll repeat it at the end of this chapter: **Remote work, done well, is great.** I've got no quarrel with the concept.

But shaming companies who don't do it doesn't sit right with me anymore, even given the arguments above.

1. Remote work exacerbates performance problems

I know it is possible for remote workers to succeed because I have watched many of them do so. Some of the people I know who have the most impact on their projects work out of coffee shops and basement offices and are well-integrated team members the whole time. Great work can happen anywhere.

But among the people I've seen struggle, a disproportionate number are remote. When I see a pattern like that, it's clear to me there's a structural issue at work. In some cases their managers and colleagues need better training. In others their communication styles don't mesh with their team properly and so expectations aren't communicated well and hand-offs are missed.

All of that can be fixed. Great remote work is never an accident; it's always a product of the organization and the employee working at it and making it better. In many organizations I've led or been part of, we have done that work and have seen great results. But I forgive a company who feel like they lack the bandwidth or expertise to do so. Telling them they *ought* to, that not doing so is a sign that they have "trust issues," seems like it sets them up to fail.

2. Remote work often creates two tiers of employee

The dominant remote-work context is a hybrid model—one or more fixed offices with significant in-person attendance, and then a remote workforce spread out geographically but collaborating with those offices. In a company like that, remote work can also hit problems around giving employees opportunity for growth.

Even well-meaning managers will fall victim to human frailties like availability heuristics when evaluating their team: a team member you share office space with will inevitably have more interactions with you, be more visible, and, as a result, be more top of your mind for new work.

Remote employees may be fine with this arrangement. I've had candidates volunteer in interviews that they *expect* to advance more slowly as a result of being remote but that the lifestyle trade is worth it for them. It's not fine with *me*. As a leader, I don't want to force-feed anyone opportunities or career paths they don't want, but I also really don't like the cultural expectation that office workers get the good stuff and remote workers swing the hammers.

It's worth mentioning that some organizations side step this by going fully virtual, no offices. One hundred percent remote. Creative Commons does this (Disclosure: I sit on their board) and, while this has its own set of costs, it certainly puts people back on a flatter plane when it comes to visibility.

3. Marginal drag matters

I consulted for a while after leaving Mozilla, and I'm sure I will again in the future, but the truth of it is that I'm not made for consulting. I really like operating. I think there's a time for strategic planning and chess games, but the days I enjoy the most are the ones when we're just getting work done in smart, focused, efficient ways. And that's what makes this piece the hardest to dodge:

Marginal wins matter.

A company *can* choose to open themselves up for remote work. It *can* bring a wealth of new talent and skills and ideas. They *can* train themselves up to manage the performance management aspects and ensure that they have good development processes in place. But if doing all that introduces drag—particularly for the first few years while they get good at it, particularly if they're a startup on a limited runway—the math just doesn't add up.

Refrain

Remote work is a wonderful thing that's more possible than ever before. I love that. If you run a company that is seriously looking at opening up to it and you're ready to make the investment, I hope that you will. If you go international the labor laws are an absolute nightmare, but even so the diversity of perspectives and talent you'll be able to attract is really exciting. I'm rooting for you.

But if you run a company that's not ready yet, you won't hear *me* call you out. I hope you'll get there some someday. In the meantime, I wish you luck. It's hard to build a thing, and as long as you're working hard to do right by your people... I'm rooting for you, too.

/19

Unlimited Vacation and Other Forms of Guilt-Based Management

The fact that you meant well doesn't make it less broken

> Johnathan

Stop me if you've heard this one before...

We're a modern company and we're blowing everything up. We don't care how many hours your butt is in a seat, we care that your work gets done. Our policy is that every employee has unlimited vacation because we trust you not to abuse it.

It's 2017 as I write this and still this line gets passed around from company to company. Maybe your company uses something like it. Maybe you're thinking about moving to this approach. I get it.

But I think it's a terrible idea.

It's not without merit, of course. Your employees and prospective employees will be pretty positive about it. It sounds amazing to people grinding it out in less *progressive* companies. You get to feel like a revolutionary. In 2008, when you'd have been among the first companies to try this, my hat would have been off to you. But it's not 2008. We know better now.

When these policies started coming out, the question was always framed in terms of whether it was wise to give people unlimited vacation, whether employees could be trusted not to overindulge in an honor system. History has suggested that yes, we can trust our employees. Anyone who manages great people for a living already knew that. It's the wrong question to ask.

The right question to ask, about vacation or any other policy, is this: Does it encourage the kind of behaviors we want in our organization? If the goal of unlimited vacation is to encourage people to take care of themselves and to take the time they need, we should ask, "Does it achieve that goal?" The answer is: No.

That's why Kickstarter walked away from it. Tribune Publishing dropped it after one week.[1] The jury's still out on whether it results in people taking more or less vacation in other shops,[2] but a consistent trend emerges nonetheless: *Your employees don't know what's okay anymore.*

Because **no one actually means "unlimited."** If I joined up and booked myself fifteen years off, I'd get a swift reality check even at such a modern employer. Even taking six months would net me a long conversation about whether that was appropriate. Instead of having an allotment they can spend largely as they see fit, your employees now have a complex tribal negotiation about how their requests stack against others, whether they're dedicated enough, and how it will reflect on them. That's complex no matter who you are, but imagine how that feels if you're a minority hire, or a woman in a male-dominated team, or in any other way not a part of the in-group at the company.

What these programs do is move your company from process-based management to guilt-based management.

Vacation decisions always involve respecting your colleagues and ensuring that your time away doesn't cause undue hardship, but when you take away a fixed pool, you invite new comparisons and competition between your people. That leads to martyrdom, burnout, and turnover. It can poison a culture.

Though I've worked with companies that offer them, and I've used them myself, I feel largely the same about rollover allowances, whereby unused vacation can carry over from one year to the next. It's easier to pressure someone not to take their planned vacation if the days aren't "lost." I haven't seen the effect be as pernicious as unlimited vacation, since there's still a fixed amount and usually a cap on rollover. But anything that invites guilt into your employee's vacation-planning process is worth scrutiny.

I believe there's a lot of exciting potential out there for more creative, respectful vacation policies. HubSpot has a mandatory minimum vacation and lets people reduce their sales quotas twice a year to make time. The RAND Corporation pays an annual bonus to employees who take all their vacation.[3] Even just planned closures (as many companies have at the end of the year) give your employees downtime they can count on and can take guilt free.

The people who advocate for unlimited vacation aren't mean-spirited. I don't think they're doing it as a culture hack to push people toward martyrdom. And I'm not asking you to give up on creative policy change or modern organizational design. I'm asking you to measure the things you care about and to be willing to admit that some things sound better than they really are.

If you're interviewing at a company with unlimited vacation, ask them how requests are evaluated and what the average time taken is. **If you run a company with unlimited vacation, benchmark how your employees are using it and pay special attention to outliers.** My prediction is that you won't find many at the "far too much vacation" end of the spectrum, but you may find quite a worrying cluster in the "far too little vacation" bucket. I'd love to be wrong about that, I hope you'll let me know if I am.

THREE

Manage Up or Manage Out

The conversations you need to have with your team, and the conversations you need to stop having.

/20

How to Be a Better Leader in 4 Badly Drawn Charts

Assholes, huggybears, and what to do about them

> Johnathan

New managers are idiots, and I was no exception. I meant well. We all do. But tech isn't great at setting examples for management, so people come in with some messed-up ideas.

I've worked with lots of managers in the years since. I've found that most green managers have one of two models for success. This was mine:

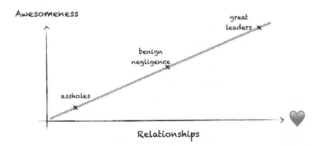

The great managers I worked with invested in the relationship. They built trust. Their deliberate listening meant that they could give me the feedback I needed to grow. Their empathy meant that they could deliver it in a way in which I could hear. I *knew* I wanted to be that kind of manager. It was *clear* to me that people in leadership positions who didn't share these values were basically bad people.

Maybe you feel this way today? There's certainly plenty of truth in it. But it's a problematic model just the same.

Some new managers, though, have a different graph in mind... with a different set of problems.

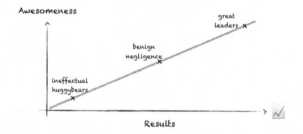

Until I figured out what was going on, talking to these people was confusing. *They* care about being good managers, too. They use similar language about building strong teams, stretching and growing. But they come to all the wrong conclusions about how to get there. Their conversations with their team are tactical and execution focused. *Their people don't blossom.* I struggled to help them see the error of their ways, and usually failed.

Good thing, too. Because I was an idiot. But so were they.

Why Are You Here?

Management's job in an organization is pretty straightforward. Chew on this framing for a second:

> A manager's job is to maximize the investment the organization makes in her team.

A company hires people to do a thing. That's an investment of time, money, and risk. The reason you're allowed to exist is because we believe you're going to help that investment pay off. That means we believe at least some of the following:

→ Your team will do more work with you holding them accountable. ✓

→ They'll align their work better with other teams through your stronger communication and coordination. ♥

→ They'll do higher-quality work with you managing and mentoring them. ♥ ✓

→ They'll do more of the right work and less of the distracting work with you focusing their efforts. ✓

→ They'll elevate the kind of work they do with you helping them grow and develop. ♥

Oh.

Relationship-oriented managers and results-oriented managers are looking at almost completely different pieces of the job. Even when they do the piece they care about brilliantly, they still fail for neglecting the rest. You can't get to great leadership by specializing exclusively in the half of this that comes naturally.

You relationship-oriented managers *do* **tend to be ineffectual huggybears.** Your teams love you, they feel nurtured and encouraged to explore and grow, they have a strong sense of team spirit, and their communication is constructive. But your focus on relationships causes you to oversoften criticism they need to hear. You protect your team from complaints that they are ineffective. When you fail to set high and clear expectations, you build teams that don't hold themselves accountable for their results.

I have seen teams so ineffective that other groups had to hire around them, teams whose management were stripped of responsibility and eventually fired. And on those managers' way out the door, I swear to you their teams wrote love letters and blog posts and poetry. That is not leadership success.

And you results-oriented assholes aren't off the hook, either. I don't dispute that you get amazing output from your team. You push them, and they respond to it. Many will even report that they appreciate it, that it makes them better. But they model themselves after you, and when you get results without empathy, they start to do the same. They are passive aggressive, or actually abusive, to others. They treat communication and empathy as weakness because they've seen how little you value it. They congratulate themselves for "just being honest."

The result is that your team ruins the productivity of everyone around them. Turnover on nearby teams multiplies dramatically. Creativity and collaboration dry up. I have seen individual results-oriented leaders drive massive turnover and toxicity before being fired themselves. It should never have gotten as bad as it did, but some people will let good results excuse a lot of bad behavior. I won't work in that environment again, and I sure as hell wouldn't call it a success, either.

Both of these styles fail. Neither maximizes the investment the company makes in their employees. These people are bad managers, and worse leaders.

An Uninspiring Compromise

Once I realized that neither end of this spectrum was a good idea, I drew the obvious conclusion:

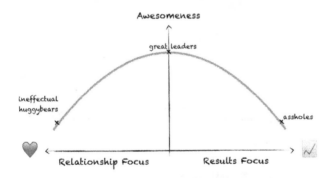

A balance of empathy and results. Hooray for symmetry! It's certainly true that huggybears become much better managers when they find ways to hold their teams accountable. It's also true that the toxicity of assholes drops when they invest at all in how they present themselves and bring others along.

There *are* people who live right in the middle of the spectrum. Of course there are. And they're delightful to work with. But my problem with this model is that I don't think this state is desirable for everyone, or even for most people. It grinds off our natural strengths in service of evenness. It's also not true that most great leaders live on that center line, so it's not clear to me that it should be a goal.

If you're at one end of the spectrum or the other, striving toward the middle is righteous. But if you're just waiting for the fourth graph, with the real punchline, here it is:

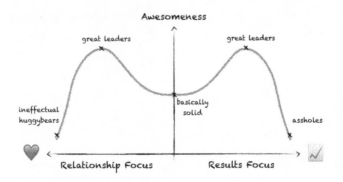

You Do You. But Do It Well.

If empathy is your strong suit, my advice is to pull yourself toward center, but not too far. Set high standards and be clear about them. Your natural ability to earn trust and respect gives you more permission than you think to be direct. Even when you have to deliver bad news, you'll do it in a way people can hear and learn from.

Ze Frank talks about how creativity flourishes when it's got something specific to do, and it's true here, too.[1] A deeper focus on results helps your people grow faster, not slower. When you tie their growth to outcomes the whole organization can see and celebrate, it reinforces the value of their work. It creates a team climate of shared accountability. *You'll love it.*

If you're driven by results, my advice is also to pull yourself toward center, but not too far. Check in with your team individually. Give them room to talk about something other than status updates. Once they realize they have room to do more than just run their list, they'll give you insights you missed. They'll take on extra work, improve pieces of the team that you don't want to tackle, and drive up the whole group's performance.

A key frustration for results-focused managers is the friction and slowness they often hit when they deal with other teams. You would be amazed how much of that disappears when you start to pay attention to how you communicate. It's a junior notion to believe that your "honest and direct" style is the only non-bullshit way to work with others. Figure out how to be heard by other teams. Bring things back to shared goals and stop trying to score points off them. Your team's productivity will skyrocket when you stop burning their bridges. *You'll love it.*

Ugh, Introspection

Managing people is hard to do well. It asks a lot from us, and no one gets there on natural talent alone. I don't think it's possible to do it well without a lot of looking inward, and I know how unpleasant that can be. But I also know that if you're a leader of people, you have figured out where you are on that graph. And you know where you ought to be next.

/21

Stop Gossiping at the Office

Resolve to silence the chatter once and for all

> Melissa

If you still run around the office whispering about your coworkers' lives and snickering in the hallways, this chapter is for you.

Let's start by stating the obvious. Gossiping *feels* good. It feels *so fucking good* to know something that other people don't know. It feels powerful to be the one who lets them in on the secret, to be the one who doles out information ... and to feel like you're getting away with something.

Here's the news flash—ready? You're not powerful, and you're not getting away with anything. You're screwing yourself, big time. Let's take a moment to break it down ...

Happy People Don't Gossip

Office gossip is a phenomenal distraction. It's fun, it's salacious, and it's utterly unrelated to you getting your actual work done. But if you are more interested in the lives of your coworkers than in your own day-to-day, there's a good chance you're unhappy about the state of your own life.

And if you don't know it, other's do. When you gossip at work, you're waving a giant fucking flag that indicates that you are unhappy—either with work or with your own life. You may not have put the flag up intentionally, but here's the g-d's honest truth:

Happy, engaged, productive people who are riding an amazing professional high don't have time to hole up in a conference room and talk about who got wasted at the accounting team's offsite. And they don't care.

It's simply not possible to be in a good, mature spot and take time out of your day to armchair-quarterback other people's life choices, fashion missteps, or accidental overindulgence at Friday's office Beer Thirty. Not happening.

Your teammates can see it. Your manager can see it. Her boss can see it, too. It doesn't matter who you're whispering to, it becomes very clear that you're distracted. And without focus, you're not operating at your professional best.

Gossiping Says More about You Than about Others

This one sounds like something your mom would say if a kid was being mean to you in the schoolyard. It's chock full of that nostalgic elementary-school wisdom that you wish was still enough to run large parts of your universe.

But life is complicated. Humans are fucking complicated. And they make things tricky that ought to be relatively straightforward.

Don't Be Mean. Don't Be Shitty. Don't Be Spiteful.

People who gossip in the office rarely think they are being mean or shitty or spiteful. They may tell themselves they are engaging in information warfare, staying in the loop, keeping a finger on the pulse of the office.

But ask anyone who has spent substantial time on the receiving end of it.[1] They will tell you it feels an awful lot like the bullshit that defined so much of middle school for so many of us.

I may have made a poor life or fashion choice on my way into the office today. Your decision to talk about my poor life or fashion choice is by far the poorer choice because . . .

People Who Gossip Have a Rep as People Who Gossip

That high you get off of knowing things that nobody else knows? That fades. You know what sticks? Having a reputation as the office gossip.

You know how people know you gossip? You told them.

Seriously. You told them when you leaned over in the meeting and whispered while your colleague was presenting. But maybe they passed that off as you making a relevant comment about the presentation.

You told them again when, unprompted, you shared someone else's news on their behalf.

You told them a third time when you convened your colleagues after hours and found the only thing to talk about was someone else's life.

However hard you think it is to ditch a reputation as the office slut, it's nothing compared to the long-term and profound professional damage of not being trusted with confidential information.

I've seen companies withhold promotions for employees with gossipy reps. And I've had it come up on reference calls for prospective employees. These folks may have no idea that they are carrying this monkey around on their back from the last job to the next job and every one thereafter. Until, that is, they resolve to put it down.

Not Your Circus. Not Your Monkey.

In my PR days, I used to have to carry a lot of confidences. Part of being ready when the *New York Times* calls for comment is having the full context. People need to tell you things, and they need to know that those things aren't going anywhere. That's how you earned trust. That's how you got access. That's how you were able to do the job and do it well.

PR teaches you when to go loud and when to stay quiet. Unless someone is paying you or has expressly solicited you to tell their story for them, best to stay quiet.

/22

The Open-Faced Shit Sandwich: Improvements on a Crappy Original

I'll be honest, this chapter has some swears

> Johnathan

Delivering negative news to someone is hard.[1] As a leader, you will spend time doing it every month. In a rough patch, you'll do it daily. It's uncomfortable. It messes with your brain's emotional centers. And it's your job.

So some bright light invented the Shit Sandwich. I don't know who. I first encountered it in *The One Minute Manager*.[2] At this point it's transcended into a management meme, like stack ranking, unlimited vacation, or Funny Hat Fridays.

The idea is to *sandwich* (get it?) your negative feedback (the 💩) before and after with positive feedback (the 🍞). Like a sandwich. Makes it easier to handle, see. Helps it not taste so bad.

It's a hilarious metaphor. You are encouraged to laugh.

It's also a load of poop. H.L. Mencken got this right 100 years ago and we've been ignoring him ever since:

There is always a well-known solution to every human problem—neat, plausible, and wrong.[3]

Ben Horowitz goes way too soft on it.[4] The shit sandwich gets held up as a clever management hack for a wide array of negative feedback scenarios. It should be dumped entirely. I've never encountered a scenario where it was the right call, and I've encountered a lot of scenarios.

Still, I get why templates can be helpful. When you're starting out, or when you encounter a new situation for the first time, having a menu of options can bring some clarity. It's a poor substitute for careful and situational communication, but I understand the appeal.

If you're going to order off the menu, then, let's check out a few of the other specials.

The Open-Faced Shit Sandwich

In the simplest, rawest case, you have to deliver some news that's really hard to handle. Maybe you're putting someone on a performance plan. Maybe they're fired. Whatever the news is, there is no way they're going to enjoy it.

In this case your goal is that the feedback be heard and complete while leaving the recipient intact enough to move forward. Don't bury it in praise. This is not a praise conversation. Doing that "shit sandwich" thing might make *you* feel better, but it sends the other person weird, mixed messages. Did the shit really matter, in the context of all that praise? What's the takeaway from that conversation, that two out of three things are going well?

You also can't just dump and run. You're about to drop a bomb on this person that will impact everything about how they relate to their work with you. It might change big pieces of their life. They are an adult, and it's fair to expect them to act as an adult. But you have the power and the context in this conversation. The pro move is to put some thought into what they'll need next, and have it ready.

Don't just hand them a pile of shit on a plate. Yes, the shit is the main feature. But give them something to hold it together, and manage through it without a giant mess.

The Shit Sundae

Not all tough feedback is so dire. In fact, the conversations I find managers most often want help with are ones about identifying and addressing a weakness. They worry that they'll lean too hard on the weakness and make it sound harsher than intended. I worry they'll lean too hard on the growth opportunity and lose the feedback about how their person is doing today.

This is basically good news. We're going to work together and make things better. Don't treat the shit as separate from the opportunity. They're integrated and don't make sense without each other. Every bite should have some of each.

Sundaes are served last. If you've done your job right, they've heard about a place where they're weak and are processing the next steps to invest and improve. You don't need to find some unrelated praise to *sandwich* this. "This isn't working but we're going to make it work together" is fine.

The Shit Shot

There's another kind of shit I see managers struggle with that's actually really easy. These are the *pro forma* conversations where you, as manager, are carrying a shitty message. The CEO doesn't like the new design. The funding didn't get approved. Someone on your team screwed up and another manager is steamed about it.

I see managers wrestle with this and try to manufacture a shit sandwich or context for the news they have to deliver. Every time I've seen it, it's been overthought.

Sometimes your org will get bad news. You will have to deliver it to your team members. They are grown-ups.

Pull them aside. Don't wait for the next one-on-one and risk that the news leaks though other channels. Don't spend a bunch of time on how you agree that things are unfair. Just pour it out in a single, clean shot. They will take it. They will probably appreciate the respect and directness. And they will move on.

Don't Manage from a Menu

All of this is a terrible idea. The right way—the *only* right way—to deliver feedback is to be thoughtful about the context and the individual and the intent of the feedback. To be a genuine human being, basically. To be a good manager, a clear communicator, and a respectful adult.

No hilarious 💩 metaphors can encompass all that. They're offered above as illustrations that shit can take many forms, but really, the whole idea is silly. Be thoughtful. Be kind. And whatever else you do, put down that sandwich.

/23

Actionable Feedback, Why It Matters, and How to Get Better at Giving It

The move from personal to professional performance evaluations

> Melissa

You're somewhere in the fourth quarter—let's say it's the first week of December. If you're in a startup, chances are good that you feel like you *just* nailed down Q4 goals. And now, before you can blink, the end of the year is upon you.

It's time for some serious reflection—on the team, on the year that was, on what's in the hopper for next year.

As you pull together the professional feedback, there's one thing nagging at you. You have feedback for a person on your team that isn't really professional feedback at all, at least not in the classical sense. It's a character flaw. And you think it's getting in the way of their success.

You don't want to go through another year without it being addressed, but there's no easy way to bring it up.

Now what?

It's Not Personal Except It's Totally Personal

For years I would get a variation of the same feedback in every performance review:

You're intimidating.

I was never sure what to do with this.

In retrospect, this was problematic feedback for a young woman in tech on a management track. But the first few times I heard it, I didn't spend much time on the gendered nature of the feedback.

I mostly just wanted to stop hearing it. I didn't stop to think about whether the feedback itself was fair or balanced.

I set about *fixing* it.

I'm loathe to admit it now, but I actually tried smiling more (yes, really). I tried using more exclamation marks in my writing. I tried incorporating smiley faces.

Perhaps unsurprisingly, it didn't work. Year after year, job after job, review after review, I got the same feedback:

You're intimidating.

I advanced in my career, I got raises and a few key promotions. But some version of that feedback was always tucked away in otherwise straightforward performance reviews.

I finally worked up the nerve to ask my manager what he meant and what he thought I might do to address it.

He explained: If people feel like they can't talk to you or if they feel scared to, you'll miss critical information that you need to do your job.

He talked about how part of the gig is understanding the organizational context, both when things are flowing and when they are not.

If your staff won't tell you when things have gone off the rails, you've got a problem. You need to get them to talk to you. And you need them to feel safe with you or they never will.

And for the *first time in my professional career*, I understood what the heck people had been trying to tell me all this time.

Mind the Gap

If you're reviewing someone who has been in the work world for a few years, there's a good chance you're about to touch a live wire.

Telling the most introverted person on your team that he needs to speak up in meetings won't go well. Not because he'll yell at you but because, worse than that, he'll nod along and say yep, he knows, and then you'll be having the exact same conversation the next year.

"Be more extroverted" is pretty much useless feedback. It's like saying "Be taller."

In my case, "Be less intimidating" was not actionable. Yes, it's closely tied to "People are scared to tell you things." But the framing of the feedback is completely different.

One version is about an elemental construct of my character. The other is about the pursuit of a business objective—context— and how it impacts me as a leader.

Get the difference?

"We need you to be different than you are" is not the same as "We need you to develop in these areas." They are related, but they come from a different starting point. And your staff are likely to be able to absorb one much more easily than the other.

Tackling the Elephant in the Room

I've done a couple of these in my time, and here's the thing I've found: telling people to work on a character attribute is sort of bullshit.

As you're prepping your review, shift the focus of your feedback from the character attribute to the intended outcome. Force yourself to dig in on *why* you want your introvert to be more vocal in meetings. Do you think you're missing a perspective? An important strategic voice? Where are you seeing the impact of this team member's quietness? The shift from personal to intended outcome lets you discuss more concrete changes in terms of how they benefit both the company and the individual.

In my case, once my manager shifted the conversation to the *impact* of me being perceived as intimidating, there was a lot more he could do to support me and a lot more I could do to address it. It was *actionable*.

I no longer felt haunted by this looming piece of annual feedback. With this context, it became clear why all the smiley faces and exclamation marks weren't helping.

/24

How I Talk to Leaders about Firing People
The reason we don't talk about it is the reason we need to talk about it

> Johnathan

I remember the first time I fired someone. Every manager does. Mine happened about a month before Christmas.

I'd managed him for six months, after inheriting him from another manager. When I got him, he was already in trouble—a remote employee nine months into his employment and with very little to show for it.

The experienced managers know what happened next. I tried to help any way I could. I bent standards and overcelebrated small successes. I gave him quick fixes to put up some wins. I was motivated, and I think he was too. Our investment paid off a little, but not enough.

We wrote up a PIP—a performance improvement plan. I hated it. It started with *This document serves as written notice that your current level of performance is unacceptable.*

Wretched. After walking him through the pieces of the PIP, he agreed it was accurate and fair. He signed it and we got to work.

At first, he was transformed. In September he picked up work left and right, interacted more with teammates than he ever had prior. He had questions, got answers, and put up code. I got feedback from his colleagues that it was great to see more from him. As his manager, it was such a relief to see his burst of energy. I had hope and he did too.

But by October, it fell apart. His pace collapsed because he'd never worked at this level before and he was exhausted. We were trying to catch him up on more than a year of development and team engagement. He missed his October targets by a wide margin.

In November, he was clear with me that he wasn't going to get anywhere close. I was clear, too. When I told him we were done, he just said, "I understand." My HR partner talked to him about the mechanics of the next week, how to return hardware and get set up with continuing medical insurance coverage. He said he felt fairly treated. I went outside and vomited in the parking lot.

It's Not about You, but It's Also about You

It's self-indulgent to focus on the hardships of managers in this. The employees being fired have the hardest time here. I don't want to diminish that. But because of that, or maybe because everyone involved just hates the whole mess, it's hard to find much good writing about firing. We're afraid to even say the word. She was *terminated*. I heard they *exited* that whole team. We *let him go*.

In the time since that first firing, I've hired many people and fired a few. I've helped managers administer their own first PIPs and, sometimes, the firing that comes at the end. I've also celebrated their PIP graduations. A solid PIP graduation is a wonderful thing. It's a second chance for an employee, their manager, and the rest of their org to do a better job working together. There's an uneasiness to them for a while, but it's happy and hopeful.

IMHO, YMMV

I don't love this Tolstoy line as much as other folks do, but it's apt here:

> Happy families are all alike; every unhappy family is unhappy in its own way.

It's hard to generalize on the subject of performance issues and firing. Every case is different, and usually the product of many screw-ups in hiring, onboarding, management, and communication. **It is far better to fix things at any of those stages—to hire well and manage well—than to find yourself here.** Still, when you do, there are some things I've found helpful to repeat to my managers and myself.

Performance Plan Theater

The worst trap I see managers fall into is thinking that performance plans are a lost cause. It's an awful, self-perpetuating loop. Not only do you guarantee that *this* PIP won't work, you then go on to teach new managers the same lesson. I've heard people senior enough to know better say that a PIP is just a tool to cover your ass and establish a paper trail on the way to dismissal. They should be ashamed of themselves.

I've dealt with labor law in a lot of different countries. It's complex; full of nuance and a significant amount of well-meaning idiocy, too. Your jurisdiction might even *require* a PIP before any termination. Regardless, it's usually at least a prudent thing to do to reduce risk. But to me that whole conversation is beside the point.

You bet on this person. You interviewed them, hired them, paid them, and introduced them to the team. They're not performing the way you expected them to, I get that, but why treat the PIP as dismal, predetermined theater? It's a tool. Use it.

Impossible Plans and Polite Passes

A good performance plan needs three basic elements. First, a clear statement that performance isn't where it needs to be. You can't dodge this piece. Second, a set of clear expectations about what success looks like—measurable and objective targets that anyone in this role ought to hit. And third, a rigorous measurement and check-in plan to track those expectations. It's a more explicit version of what any good manager should be doing anyhow.

My two tests for any PIP a manager puts in front of me are these:

1. **Is it impossible?** Do I believe that this PIP can succeed? Is there a clear definition of success, and is it in keeping with the expectations of the role we hired this person to fill?

2. **Is it a polite pass?** Will a person who graduates this PIP be back to a clean bill of health? I don't want someone to squeak through and wear it for the rest of their time on our team. If you graduate and sustain that level of performance, you should be back firmly in the "solid" camp.

A PIP that passes those tests can be written by any manager who cares about seeing their employees succeed. If you *can't* write a PIP that does, then a performance plan isn't the right tool for your situation. A PIP can't solve "We hired marketing too early and don't know what to do with them," or "We don't handle remote very well." A PIP also can't solve "I don't like you."

Start Early

Managers who haven't fired are usually afraid of it. They should be—it's no fun. But the fear makes them do a dumb thing: it makes them delay. Waiting makes everything worse, because the problems deepen and the hope of recovery fades.

When a manager tells me that a member of their team is under-performing, I start a clock. Poor performance can come from a lot of places and is often pretty easy to correct with a single direct conversation. Usually that conversation, in a regular one-on-one, pulls out something situational—maybe not even related to their work. Life happens and, as Melissa says, "People bring their whole selves to work." In those cases, the performance is self-correcting and I cancel the clock. In most other cases, the problem *is* work-related but honest conversation identifies changes we can make or expectations that we can correct. And again, I cancel the clock.

But if a direct conversation yields little change and a month later we're in the same spot, it's time. **Remember, a PIP is not a firing.** A PIP is a tool to either bring performance into line with the expectations or confirm that this employee isn't going to meet those expectations. There can be a hundred reasons for that, but none of them are helped by maintaining the status quo.

A one-month clock followed by a three-month PIP means that before an employee is fired there would have been at least four months of poor performance. In truth, it's often more like six to nine months, as managers will try a few approaches to performance management before resorting to a PIP. Some employment cultures (Japan and France both come to mind) consider this insufficient, but in North America in general, and in a startup context in particular, six months of poor performance is already a long time—hard for the team, hard for the manager, and hard for the employee. It's selfish to drag that out because of your own discomfort.

You're Not Off the Hook

Lots of employee departures can be mutual and positive and can happen for the right reasons, but a firing is almost always the result of some screw-ups. Even if you manage the process well, it shouldn't ever feel good to reach that point.

How did someone get nine months into their employment with so little work done and so little team integration? If he was never going to work out, then we made several errors in hiring. If we were right to hire him, then we clearly messed up onboarding and integration. In either case we let problems get far too deep before addressing them. We screwed up as a management team, but he's the one that got fired.

There's a deep unfairness to the fact that poor performance can be multidimensional but that employees bear the brunt of the consequence. Yes, our employees are grown-ups and should be capable of a degree of communication and self-management. Yes, they have a responsibility to ask questions if expectations aren't clear. But as leaders and managers of managers, we should wear it every time an employee is fired. Whether you buy the *servant leadership* stuff or not, you have a power over the people on your team that you should feel, every day, like you have to earn.

/25

A Brief Overview of Failing, Firing, and Scotch
(FFS for short)
> Melissa

We're sitting around the living room drinking super-smoky Laphroaig Quarter Cask and talking about the first time we had to fire someone. One of our friends works in HR. She's recounting terminations from her early career (without specific details, of course) and grimacing.

I tell her about the first time I had to fire someone. I was so nervous that the HR guy in the room did most of the talking (still grateful!). When it was over, I went to the women's bathroom and threw up. The person I fired hit a pole on the way out of the office parking lot. A small fender bender but still, pretty disastrous.

I sit there, cross-legged on my couch, ten years smarter, and I'm overwhelmed by how many things I wish I'd known then.

Why You're Failing at Your Job
Someone once told me that people fail in their jobs for one of three reasons: **Attitude, Aptitude,** or **Skills.** Sometimes they fail for more than one reason, but if things aren't working, it's usually at least one.

Attitude is how you show up for the job. Sometimes people get in their own way. Sometimes you get a new boss and that person rubs you the wrong way. Sometimes someone else gets the promotion you thought you'd earned and you feel grumpy. Sometimes you never liked the job but took it because you needed the money or didn't feel like you had other options.

Attitude is pretty straightforward. It's not that you can't do the job or learn to do the job. It's that you don't want to.

And I hear you saying, well, I would want to if I'd gotten that promotion. Or I would want to if my boss weren't such a jackass. Or if I didn't have to work on the lamest projects, or with idiotic team members. Maybe that's true. But...

If your rider for coming to work excited to get shit done includes a bunch of things being different than they currently are, your attitude is likely standing in the way of you being successful in your role.

Aptitude is about whether you are capable of doing the role you are in. Do you have the smarts to do the job? Can you learn? This isn't simply a case of whether you are clever or quick, this is about how you adapt to the needs of the business.

Are you one step ahead? Can you (as Canadians are fond of saying) skate to where the puck is going to be?

This is about problem solving, troubleshooting, understanding the business and optimizing for success. Expectations of aptitude will vary from organization to organization and from role to role.

Skills is often about training. When skills are a problem, sometimes it's because an employee is being asked to do something they've never done before or that wasn't explicit in the job description. This is particularly common in early-stage startups where many of the first hires are generalists.

You were hired as a marketing manager because you could manage social media and pull together great campaigns, but when the company pivots to enterprise sales, you now need a really different playbook. Suddenly it doesn't matter that you are a solid B2C generalist, you find yourself totally out over your skis.

The good news is that if attitude and aptitude are in a solid spot, skills is the easiest of the three to resolve. This can take a variety of forms—mentors, classes, informal or professional coaching. There are many ways to train up on new skills.

Okay, Time to Put Our Boss Hat On

As the manager, once you can pinpoint the disconnect, next steps should come into focus. If you're staring down a combo of attitude and aptitude mismatch or attitude and skills, I feel for you. It's hard enough to help someone develop their professional skills when conditions are optimal, never mind when they are struggling to be vulnerable enough to accept your feedback.

You can spend a bunch of cycles stressing about how to share the feedback so the person can hear it, worrying about hurting their feelings, and scenario-testing how they might respond. If that's where you are right now, I have some news for you …

If it's not working for you, it's not working for them either
It took a while for me to understand the two-sided nature of employment. Everyone always says, "It's not only that they're

interviewing *you*—you're interviewing *them*, too." That turns out to be true for more than just the interview phase. It's true for the annual review phase, too.

Your employee who struggles with attitude doesn't feel good about how they are showing up at work. They may have a long list of reasons that focus on their context and not their own actions, but in the quiet moments of self-reflection, they know this isn't sustainable.

Everyone deserves an opportunity to be awesome

If it's not at your company or it's not in that role, the kindest thing you can do is give someone a firm nudge toward finding a role where they *can* do amazing things. It *sucks* to go to work every day and feel like you're phoning it in, you struggle to get through the day, or you are otherwise mismatched to your work.

When you let someone go, you give them an opportunity to reset their day-to-day and find something that's a better fit. Okay, this may sound a bit Pollyannaish, but consider this: In the short term, it feels awful—like someone is breaking up with you. In the long term, you are saving both the company and the employee from years of being stuck in an unhappy marriage.

Organizations are self-healing

You want this to be false, especially if you believe in tenure and you feel that being in the same place for a long time should count for something. It does, but probably not for the things you think. It counts in that you've mastered an old version of the organization.

You want this to be false if you're a superhero and you feel like you are the only person who can save the organization. You want it to be false if you feel like without you, everything will come crashing down.

You want this to be false because the other version sounds really heartless. It cuts dangerously close to people being unimportant and interchangeable and replaceable.

This isn't about swapping out cogs. This isn't an empathy-free approach to human resources. This is about the first rule of full-time employment: *Help the business succeed.* This is about not tanking the group to save the individual—it's about optimizing for the team and the organization's wins.

There is a point where it's clearly not going to work out because of a failure in attitude, aptitude, or skills (or some combination thereof). This is about the decision not to sit in that space, not to stay in that space, not to quietly hope that the situation will improve on its own, that the person will find another job, that they will understand the subtext and address the root causes on their own.

As a new manager, I dreaded letting someone go. I would feel a small knot in my stomach and I would carry it with me. I prayed for passive resolution that didn't require any action on my part.

In my retrospective of all the past terminations I've either conducted, been part of, or been on the receiving end of, one thing sticks out:

I never regretted pulling the trigger; I regretted not having done it sooner.

Failing sucks. Firing someone sucks. Getting fired sucks.

If you have to go through any or all of it, I hope ten years out you find yourself with Laphroaig in hand, surrounded by friends who have lived through it too.

/26

Why You Should Never Apologize for Crying in the Office

Why is yelling fine but crying is out of bounds?

> Melissa

Oh, tech...You adorable, idealistic, inconsistent beast! Tell me again about how much you value passion.

Let's talk about the workers who stay at the office so they qualify for free dinner.[1] Let's laugh about the time your whole team got baked at the office with Snoop Dogg.[2] Let's recount the zillion other times you celebrated the blurring of professional and personal boundaries.

As an industry, we have limitless appetite for these stories. They are the folklore of modern tech companies. We lean on passion as a core value for tech workers, but we are highly selective in our recounting of these stories. We must be passionate about our work to the exclusion of other aspects of life (relationships, dining at home, sleeping, etc.), but we never talk about how being passionate about our work means being *emotional* about it.

This seems so strange—that we show up with passion in spades but are meant to leave all other feelings at the door.

Be passionate, but heaven forbid you're sad or upset or overwhelmed when a high-stakes project doesn't turn out as planned.

Passion Is Inherently Emotional

Tech leans on passion as a positive, but the minute someone cries, suddenly it's all "Can someone call for leaky eye socket cleanup in the third-floor conference room?"

As an undergrad, I landed a paid internship with a huge multinational company. It was a big deal. It was a make-or-break-your-career-type gig, and the role was exactly what I'd been studying in school. Except when I started the job, I realized there was a huge gap between theory and practice.

I was working alongside people who had spent their *whole careers* in the field. I had passion out the yang, but I had very few practical office skills.

I spent those early days on the verge of tears, terrified that I'd embarrass myself in front of my professional heroes. Every day for the first two weeks, I went home and cried.

At my core, I cared about doing a good job. I was passionate about the industry and I had a lot riding on that internship. I lucked into some amazing mentors and by the start of the third week, life started to get much better. I was able to understand (at a basic level) how what I was learning in school applied to the workplace. I started to find my groove.

Crying at Work vs. Crying about Work

I've had people from all walks of life cry in one-on-ones. The first thing they usually do is look up, red-cheeked, and then look down at the floor and apologize.

"I'm sorry. I'm fine. Really, I'm fine. It's okay. I'm just..."

When I first started managing people, I didn't really know what to do. If I'd been more experienced, I probably could have sensed it coming. But in the early days, I was caught off guard more than once.

We'd be in the middle of a discussion about a project or a program or something totally unrelated and suddenly, the person I'm talking to is crying.

Shit. Now what?

The first few times someone cried in a conference room with me, I froze. I waited for them to finish then I rushed to get back to neutral and unemotional ground as quickly as possible.

After a couple years of managing people, a pattern started to emerge.

There were people who were *crying about work*. Work is often where passion and emotion are closely linked. These folks take it to heart when a project isn't working out or when they are stressed about missing a deadline. They are invested in the organization's success, and they hold themselves to a high standard.

And then there were people who were *crying at work about totally non-work things*. These folks had a whole bunch of life happening outside of work, things that didn't disappear just because they walked into the office.

We Bring Our Whole Selves to Work

The *at work/about work* breakdown helped me understand this:

We bring our whole selves to work.

If you have a sick parent, that emotional load comes with you to the office. If your kid is having a hard time at school, it's on your mind. If you got cut off in traffic, annoying and insignificant as it might be, that too contributes to your emotional state when you sit down at your desk.

My two weeks of crying at the big multinational? My internship started two weeks before my summer sublet was available. I'd decided to crash with friends and commute from the end of the subway into downtown every morning. I am not a morning person.

Was I upset because the internship was kicking my ass and I was trying to learn a whole slew of new skills all at once? Yes. Was I also out of sorts because of stuff in my personal life? Yes.

There are people who are crying about work, and there are people who are crying at work about non-work things. For both groups, it's important to recognize that *it's all intermixed*. Because we're humans. And emotional complexity is what we humans do.

There's No Need to Apologize

This idea that we show up at work as complete and emotionally integrated people isn't novel, but it was a breakthrough management moment for me. I no longer wanted to run from tears in one-on-ones. I wasn't afraid. I wasn't uncomfortable.

And I no longer felt like people had anything to apologize for.

So I started with that. When people were looking at their feet, I'd make eye contact and say, "You don't have anything to apologize for."

No Seriously, Don't Apologize

We have all these hangups and stereotypes about what workplace tears mean. We have this idea that crying is weak, that there's no place for it in an office. The more time I spent with this idea, the more I found myself wondering about all the other types of behavior that we condone in tech.

Where did we get this idea that yelling in an office is fine but crying is way out of bounds? How is it that when my former boss punched a wall in anger, he felt no compunction to apologize for lashing out, but when one of the recent grads on my team starts to well up, she's instantly embarrassed and apologetic?

Getting high in the office, punching walls, yelling … Tears seem like the *least* of our problems.

Except tears are gendered. So is yelling. So is punching.

Women—young women in particular—are more likely to be the ones crying in the office. And older men are more likely to be the ones perpetuating overt aggression in the office. One of these creates a hostile work environment. The other does not.

Do not apologize for your tears. You have nothing to apologize for. The only reason you feel like you do is because of a legacy of gender bias in the workforce. This bias was designed to overvalue hypermasculine traits.

You bring your whole self to work. Your ability to feel sad or overwhelmed or upset is what keeps you from throwing chairs when the going gets tough.

Crying isn't weak. Punching walls is.

/27

What Happens in the Rooms with No Windows
I have a thing to tell you, but you have to promise to keep it quiet

> Johnathan

Every office has them. In Mozilla's Castro Street offices, it was room "3s—Strong Bad." I made lots of trips to California in those days. I sat in lots of meeting rooms. I knew which ones had spare MacBook power adapters and which ones got hot in the afternoon when the sun came in. I knew that there was only one reason someone would ask to meet in room 3s *specifically*.

3s was the only room on that floor with no window to the hallway. 3s was where you went when you wanted to cry.

You Might Have Fucked Up
When a coworker starts to cry, it's natural to freak out. If you're new to this and it's just happened for the first time and you manage this person (and they're no longer in the room)... go ahead. Freaking out is a mostly healthy empathic response and it's possible those tears are a sign that you have screwed things up badly.

How you resolve that is a whole different book than the one we're writing today, though. In the meantime, just do everything Ijeoma Oluo says: Apologize like a grown-up.[1]

But You Probably Haven't

Truth be told, most of the tears I've seen at work had nothing to do with me. They were from people not even in my organization. Sometimes people just need to cry and have someone listen.

> People bring their whole selves to work. We tell them to. We talk about passion and dedication. We celebrate their heroics. We ask them to go above and beyond. We shouldn't be surprised when that overflows.

I've had people in rooms without windows cry about problems in their marriage, dying family members, dying pets, harassment from an ex-boyfriend, romances with other employees, quitting jobs, hating their manager, overwork, wanting different work, wanting to move, and more than once for reasons they wouldn't or couldn't tell me.

I've even had people tell *me* not to freak out, that they cry when they're working something out and that I shouldn't think more of it than that. Crying is just part of their process. And that's okay.

This Isn't High School

For me—and I bet for many of you—teary people come naturally. In high school I'd always have friends who *needed to talk*.

I have a thing to tell you but you have to promise to keep it quiet.

I'd always agree. I wanted to be helpful. I think, by and large, I kept those confidences, too. It's nice to feel trusted. And why wouldn't you listen if that's all your friend needs?

Now I'm in tech, and what I've seen is that startups and other high-intensity employment build strong relationships quickly. When your colleagues are also friends, it seems cold to maintain professional boundaries. It can feel a lot like high school.

But you are not in high school. And running the same relationship scripts you did in high school is a mistake with real consequences.

You Are About to Fuck Up

Ever been deposed? I have, and you don't want to be. It's no fun. It's lawyers and voice recorders in a conference room that's too hot. It's mundane, repetitive questions that jump around and backtrack. It's poking at you from different angles to see if your story is consistent. It's surprise questions about your personal life that you don't even have to answer, that seem designed just to put you on edge or to make you feel guilty. It's wondering about the story behind every question.

And between questions it's quiet. Just the scratch of pencils making extensive notes about what you've said. Someone pouring lukewarm coffee into a mug. Someone asking if you're ready to continue.

This is true even when you aren't part of the thing being investigated. I can only imagine that if I had known actual details, it would have gone much worse. It doesn't take much imagination to realize how much *more* awful the experience was for the people involved.

So let's talk about those secrets again.

By the Time You've Heard It, It's Too Late

It turns out that when you're not in high school, some confidences are hard to keep. Many states require any report of harassment, assault, or hostile work environment to be investigated. I'm not a lawyer, but I've had more than one remind me and my managers that failure to report isn't just a liability for the company, but a personal liability for me as a member of management.

I believe pretty strongly that any action in such a case should be driven by what the victim needs. But my belief doesn't change local labor law, and neither does yours. If whatever this secret is hits the light of day and you're found to have concealed it, it will not go well for you. And the legal machine is likely to trudge forward whether the victim wants it to or not.

I understand the desire to be helpful, but when someone says, "I have a thing to tell you but you have to promise to keep it quiet," just stop for a minute. Think before you say "Of course." Taking that information on and then at some point sharing it with others revictimizes this person you are trying to help.

Do you actually intend to lie under deposition? I'm a pretty clever fellow, but even if I wanted to I don't think I could have kept up a set of false denials that long. It's an utterly exhausting process. If you *don't* plan to, then you owe it to them to be honest up front: "I want to help any way I can, but I understand that part of being a manager here is that I have to report some things whenever I hear them." Let them decide whether they can accept that or not.

You can tell me you don't like that—that it's less fun, and sounds officious, and hurts rapport. I don't like it much either. But it's not really about what you or I think, and denial doesn't help. You're not in high school; the stakes are higher. And the only thing worse than not being there for someone who's been victimized is setting them up to be victimized *again* so that you can feel better in the moment.

Postscript

People still want to cry sometimes, and I still listen. I still want to help, and I feel fortunate and honored that it's something people trust me with. I do warn people up front which things I have to act on, and it probably does put some distance between us that I wish we didn't need.

If you're one of those people, or if you're someone with a secret, I hope you'll find your support. And if your secret is the kind of thing that should be reported, I hope you'll find the strength to do so, and that your management team listens, investigates, and believes you. I know that's a lot to hope for, and I understand if you just can't.

God, people are tough.

/28

Your New Process Is No Substitute for Giving a Shit

The lesson every Starbucks barista has already learned

> Johnathan

To be fair, someone at IBM *tried*.

I worked at IBM for a few years after university, and it was clear that someone meant well. Management at the local team level was always hit or miss. Somebody knew it, and they put in place two processes to fill in the gaps left by that weak leadership.

Or so they thought.

First was the **Personal Business Commitments** document. (For IBMers, the PBC. Everything at IBM is an acronym. Including "IBM.") In a large organization you can lose track of how your work matters. And knowing how your work matters is critical to keeping you engaged and creative.[1]

Your PBC supported this need for context. It was a personalized set of commitments to the business—from your own, through your team's, all the way to IBM's global strategy. It connected the dots and showed you why your work was an important piece of the machine.

Second was the **Individual Development Plan** (IDP). IBM wanted to invest in our growth, we were told. Each employee would develop this plan alongside our manager. Both of us would be held accountable for its completion.

PBCs and IDPs. Individualized, and built in to your accountability with your team.

Doesn't that sound lovely?

Lies, Damned Lies, and Process Metrics

Here's how it actually worked in my department.

My PBC said, "*Develop and release WebSphere Application Developer Integration Edition.*" That's it. That's the whole thing. I never saw other people's PBCs, but there must have been eight to a hundred of us working on WSADIE. I have the distinct impression that they all said the same thing.

In time I learned that my IDP was a tool I could control, and I took more ownership over my own management. But for the first few years, my IDP said, in its entirety, "*On the job training and peer mentoring as appropriate.*" I suspect that here, too, I was not alone. I saw no evidence that my managers were ever brought to task on this stuff. Honestly, I bet their IDPs and PBCs were more of the same.

Process won't make your people care if they don't care.

This is not unique to IBM. I remember a few years ago Starbucks rolled out a customer satisfaction program. Do you remember this, too? Their systems were set up to print a survey invite for one in every ten customers or so. Fill out a satisfaction survey, get a free drink code. And Starbucks HQ applied a lot of pressure on stores to score well.

I saw at least three stores adopt the same approach to this process. When the survey invites printed off, the staff would stash them instead of handing them over. They'd save them for their friendly regulars. They got a lot of perfect scores, and their regulars got a lot of free drinks.

It's the same at my auto shop. The business gets so much pressure to ace their feedback scores that they have a five-step phone and email cadence for every visit. Not about how our service experience *actually went*—purely as a plea to score them perfectly on the survey. If you've ever had an Uber or Lyft driver ask for five stars, you know the drill.

This is not what the creators of these processes intended.

But We Need More Structure!

Process itself isn't the problem. Well-structured processes help well-run companies avoid mistakes and optimize. Good pilots use checklists. Smart companies schedule regular compensation reviews. Blind candidate screens are great process. So are one-on-ones.[2]

Yay, process!

But any time you introduce a new process, ask yourself why. What are you trying to do with it? I find the answers usually fall into one of two buckets:

1. **Process as visibility/systematicity/error avoidance/risk management.** Some examples: We should review core metrics weekly so that we're all on the same page about how we're doing. We should have a checklist before pushing new code to production because we sometimes forget steps. We should standardize interview questions and scoring to reduce bias.
2. **Process as driver of organization or individual change.** We need a scoring system for prioritizing feature work because we're too scattered. We need mandatory career plans for every employee because they feel adrift.

Most organizations need the stuff in bucket #1 as they grow. Adding people strains old communication and coordination channels. When that happens, it's a good instinct to write down the things you used to keep in your head. Most orgs go through an adolescence during which they overinvest in these processes. The result is rigidity and loss of velocity, but usually people who care will call it out and pull things back to center.

The stuff in bucket #2 is much more dangerous, especially for small organizations. People are complex, and organizations are just *full* of them (see Chapter 1). Process can't drive meaningful and lasting change on its own; only other people can do that. When I hear someone ask for an automatic scoring system for product ideas, I ask where product leadership went. When I hear people demand a scripted career process, I ask what their managers are doing.

Process to help you connect with your leaders or report your leaders' failings or hold your leaders accountable? Yes. Yes to all of those! But process can't replace leadership. Process supports leadership by catching the edge cases, watches for human frailties, and provides escalation paths for bad judgment.

If you are trusting to process things that you should trust to judgment, you have a leadership problem. More process won't make that go away.

Employees rally around calls for more process as a way to remedy some of the power imbalance—to mitigate the damage of decisions made without care. Maybe they just don't understand the decisions being made, but often they don't trust the integrity of the decision makers.

It sucks. And if you're an employee caught in that trap and unable to vote with your feet, I have only sympathy for your situation. I don't think process will give you the wins you want, but I understand the desperation to find a fix.

If you're a leader hearing these calls in your company, you have some hard work to do to understand what your people need. Are they asking for process to support your judgment, or are they asking for process because they don't trust your judgment? And what have you done to earn, or undermine, that trust? And what are you going to do about it now?

This is a moment to lead. Show up for them. Give a shit. Make things better. Do it with your own authentic integrity and commitment, not with an acronym.

FOUR

Leading When It's Hard

Hard lessons about growing up without forgetting who you are

/29

Leadership Is Not About Your Good Intentions

Managing junior vs. senior staff, and why you might be an ass

> Johnathan

I don't honestly remember which Mike it was. But early in my life as a manager at Mozilla, I remember Mike Shaver (or maybe Mike Beltzner, or Mike Connor, or Mike Schroepfer) said a thing that was formative for me. I've held on to it since.

> Junior people we evaluate on effort.
> Senior people we evaluate on outcomes.

It would be a mistake to have this as the only tool in your management arsenal (Who decides when you switch? Does this imply that the ends justify the means? Shouldn't junior folks care about outcomes?), but it's a pretty solid piece of the puzzle.

There are two ways to read it. The first is to read it directly as a management rule about expectations and results. The second is to see it as a revelation about why you are an ass. But let's not get ahead of ourselves.

First Reading: Manage Different People Differently
Strategies

A great junior employee brings energy, knowledge, and new ideas. What they often lack is an understanding of how to get things done in an organization. My cognitive psych books would call this a lack of cognitive strategies. Strategies are meta-knowledge, the tools you pick up as you learn that help break down certain kinds of problems.

For a five-year-old, this might be learning that you can use your fingers to visualize addition problems. For a new engineering hire, it's learning how to trace one call path as a way to understand a new pile of code.

As you get more seasoned, your strategies bias toward social and business problems instead of cognitive ones. You learn how to run a meeting, and how to pre-flight the important decisions before that meeting even starts. You learn strategies for tracking outstanding work and follow-ups. You come to realize how much of your success is tied up in getting things done instead of having great ideas.

And one day you realize you're not junior anymore.

Best intentions

Holding a junior employee accountable for the success of the organization isn't realistic. Without those strategies, they don't know how to make success happen. So we substitute in productivity goals, progress goals. Are you writing clean code? Are you collaborating well? Did you hit your OKRS?

We evaluate junior folks on their efforts and their intentions. If they did hard, diligent work on a doomed project, it's hard to make its dooming their fault. I know some cultures disagree. They feel that you should leave a team you don't believe in.[1] That you should speak up early and boldly.

I've worked in those cultures. They're not what you want to build. When you're new it's hard to know the difference between a bad idea, a good idea with the wrong team, and a good team with a bad plan. It encourages people to be hairtrigger and awful to each other as a way to seem smart. It encourages other people to leave. Don't do it.

Junior people we evaluate on effort.

No easy buckets

But outcomes still matter. The buck has to stop. I've seen companies that score everyone on effort, but I've never seen *great* companies that do so. Every company needs a set of folks who *do* understand the context. Who *can* be held accountable for the right things actually getting done.

That's what executives are for. You are the people who turn strategy into execution. It's a hard job. It's why you get a fancy title and a high salary and a team of people. You need to prioritize, spot problems early, adapt and adjust. You need to empower your teams to be creative but never step so far away that you lose the thread of how they'll get it done. As the man says, you have to keep your nose to the grindstone while lifting your eyes to the hills.[2]

And you get zero points for effort.

If your team works hard on goals you set and they don't move the business forward, *you* messed up. If they fail to hit a target because you distracted them with shifting priorities, it doesn't matter what your intentions were. If you re-org your business in ways that make sense to you but confuse and paralyze your people, you don't get points for meaning well.

Senior people we evaluate on outcomes.

And if that's all you take from this chapter, it's still a good rule. But ...

Second Reading: You Are an Ass

Here's a funny thing. A lot of you execs, in tech and elsewhere, will nod vigorously with all that up there. It supports the mythology of the long-suffering executive. It reinforces that you are the *results*-bearers. The *doers*. Hooray for you.

But then a week from now, I'll see you somewhere and you'll say something breathtakingly moronic. Something like "They couldn't have picked a better headshot, lol?" in a profile of a woman CEO. Or asking, on a panel, "Don't you think that women founders just pitch differently and that's why they don't get funded as often?" Or giving an interview where you solemnly explain, "I don't see color when I look at candidates. We're a meritocracy."

You'll say this stupid thing and then, if you're lucky, someone will call you on it. They'll tell you it's offensive, and ignorant, and discriminatory. And what will you say? You, the buck stop? You, the owner of outcomes?

"Oh, come on. That's not what I intended."

Really? *Really?* It's such a junior move to say that you meant something else, that you weren't trying to offend. As though that makes it all better. Of course you weren't *trying* to offend. I'd hope not!

Your employees aren't *trying* to fail, either. But if they're suitably senior, you hold them accountable for that failure just the same. *We just talked about this. You just agreed.*

You're being an ass, right now. If you want to be a leader, own it. Like you would anywhere else in your life. Work harder to understand the context, develop better strategies for anticipating and avoiding future failure—the stuff you expect junior folks to do. Because I see you, and you're sure as shit not acting very senior right now.

/30

Why Is Your Team So Angry All the Time?

If you show up to work looking for a fight, you'll find one

> Melissa

I Learned It by Watching You

In the late eighties, there was a reasonably famous anti-drug commercial. Maybe you've seen it. Or maybe you weren't born yet, in which case I feel old. Thanks for that.

A father busts into his son's room and confronts him with a cigar box. He wants to know where his kid got the pot, and he wants to know where he got the idea that it was okay to do drugs. The kid, flustered, blurts out: "I learned it by watching you!"

The commercial doesn't hold up over time. The reactions from the dad are choppy; the overacting from the kid, comical. The whole thing seems very silly thirty years later. But it touches on something most seasoned leaders know:

You manifest what you model.

Your people are not only watching your every move, they are *emulating* you. And, unfortunately, you don't get to pick and choose which parts they copy.

If you're a collaborative leader who values consensus, there's a good chance you see this reflected in your team. They solve problems together. They are collegial and respectful when they disagree. And while they don't always move super fast, they have a good foundation for getting to positive outcomes.

However, we're not always the best versions of our selves. You bring your whole self to work (see Chapter 26), even when you aren't feeling collaborative or teamy (Chapter 3).

There are times when you are downright pissed off. When you're angry that a project isn't going well, or frustrated that your consensus-loving team is taking a month to design a new feature (Chapter 36). There are times, quite frankly, when you will *lose your shit* as a leader.

And in these shit-losing moments, the exact same elements apply. Your team pays attention. They watch you. They watch the leaders around you. They notice everything. They wait for what happens next.

The Microscope of Leadership

Humans are funny little monkeys. If there's a monkey in charge, we watch that monkey more than the others. We are curious about that monkey. And we pick up our cues about how we should behave from that monkey.

Leading a large team of people can feel like being on your own reality TV program. The cool part is that folks are paying attention. They want to know what's on your mind, how you feel about a particular project, or the backstory behind a recent leadership decision.

But there are other, less cool, parts.

Let's say your team is crunching on a bunch of deadlines all at once. And you are stressed. Not little *s* stressed. Capital *S*, capital *everything* STRESSEDDDDD. (The *D*'s at the end are for extra stress.)

In a team meeting, you ask for updates on a cross-functional initiative. Your team relies on another team to move things forward. Bad news: the other team hasn't done their part.

Fuck, you say in your head.

That team is so useless, you say out loud.

Your team was paying attention before. They caught the part where you were fired up about an initiative. They caught the eyebrow arc when you wanted to know more about that engineering estimate. And they for sure caught that last bit where you trashtalked another department.

And now, as the saying goes, It. Is. On.

My Team vs. Everybody

Does your team seem stressed out? A little crispy at the edges? Are they fumbling the easy and obvious stuff? Are those little fumbles turning into bigger fumbles? Are you fighting other departments instead of your competitors?

Uh oh ... You're in trouble.

Just like your wins compound (see Chapter 35), so do your losses. Pretty soon, you've got a team that not only can't work together, you've got a team that *doesn't want* to work together.

The departments splinter off to make their own mini teams, each with their own culture and leader. And those leaders, when asked about other teams, reinforce your combative culture.

That team is so useless.

Once your team stops trusting other teams, they start trying to solve all problems on their own. Pretty soon, you find that distinct teams are hiring for redundant functions. Marketing has their own web development organization so they don't have to ask web dev for support. Your product team now has their own copywriter. Before you know it, HR has hired a graphic designer.

Your leaders teach their teams not to rely on other teams. They can't scale. The people on those teams are angry.

They are working twice as hard as everyone else. They are doing it all themselves. And they have no idea what the hell those other departments even do.

But, hey, *they* didn't hire 'em ...

If you are panicked about an upcoming board meeting, so is your team. If you think it's okay to snipe at your executive assistant, don't be surprised to see your staff sniping at each other.

And when you look up and find yourself with a team of people who won't work together, don't trust each other, and make decisions from a reactionary place? You won't have anyone else to blame.

They learned it from watching you.

/31

Bullies, Bylines, and That Other B Word
The relationship between seniority and likability

> Melissa

In hushed tones my stepdaughter asks me if a word that she's heard at school is a bad word.

I don't believe in bad words. I assess the merit of individual words based on whether that word does a good or bad job of communicating what someone is trying to convey. I disagree with my stepdaughter's fundamental premise that language is binary, that words fall squarely into two camps, either good or bad.

She's six. This is a chewy response for a six-year-old, so I don't tell her this.

Instead I say, well, the word you're asking about is a word that bullies use when they want to be mean to someone. So no, it's not a very nice word, and used in the way you're describing, it's likely to hurt someone's feelings.

I sidestep the entire inherently good vs. bad dilemma. Perhaps that's a conversation for when she's seven.

• • •

I love language. I spend more cycles than the average human on word nerdery. I love the challenge of finding exactly the right words to communicate a concept or express an idea.

For all my love of words, I also value precision. My professional reputation around editing is much more machete than scalpel. Looking back at past writing, I cringe where I'm unnecessarily wordy, rewriting whole passages in my head as I read. This emphasis on precision is sometimes misinterpreted.

I'm 14. I pick up the phone at my grandma's house. One of her friends is calling. I take a message and say I'll let my grandma know she called. The friend later tells my grandma that I am "curt." (This is a pretty deep burn from an octogenarian to a teenager.)

Some variation of this feedback has followed me for basically my whole life.

So I work at it. I work at softening and smoothing the rough edges. I read over my professional emails before they go out. I read and then reread the grumpy emails to make sure I've captured what I want to say before hitting Send.

The entire early part of my career was spent steeped in this stuff: which message for which audiences, why those over other words…Years of deliberate practice has made me better at it. I don't get it right every time, but it's been a long time since anyone accused me of being curt.

When I get to Canada, I go to meetings and at the end, invariably, the person I'm meeting with says, "Wow, thanks for such a direct conversation." I come home excited, thinking the meeting has gone well. My Canadian husband has to explain the cultural subtext—that people are gently teasing me.

• • •

It's spring. My younger daughter is happily babbling next to me and I'm talking to a former employee who is ostensibly over to visit the baby, but as we start to catch up, it's clear there's something else on her mind.

She's been out of school a few years and is thinking about the next step in her career. She's in her element as an individual contributor. She likes the self-reliance of this type of work, but as her skills have grown, she's increasingly interacting with other teams, the managers of other teams, and she's trying to navigate how to get what she needs without having direct authority over her colleagues. They don't report to her. She is younger and less experienced than many of them.

Ah. *This* is why she's here.

And so I explore the space a bit. I ask questions without jumping to a solution or a conclusion.

"What would it feel like to count on your coworkers?" I ask. "What would it look like to have to call them out if you weren't getting what you needed? How might you design the hand-off points to hold each other accountable without direct reporting authority? And what about this is scary?"

"I—" She pauses. "I don't want them to call me a bitch." She whispers the last word.

I stop. I know that feeling. I have spent years in this exact space. Maybe my whole life.

"What if…," I ask. "What if they already have?"

She stops.

I continue. "This is one of the things that sucks for women in leadership. There is an inverse relationship between seniority and likability. The higher you go, the less likable your coworkers will find you."

"What if," I say, "the thing between you and the next phase of your career is on the other side of that? What if you haven't found your boss voice because you want to be liked? What would it look like to know that's a possibility and press ahead anyway?"

The baby kicks her feet wildly against her bouncy chair. The sun is moving across the backyard and soon it will time to get her ready for bed.

• • •

When you work in PR, you're mostly trained to be behind the camera or, in the event that you find yourself in front of it, to be a neutral mouthpiece for the organization or company you represent. You are the person asking everyone else to put "my views are my own" at the end of their Twitter bio, lest that cat GIF be confused for an official statement.

I spent years crafting messages for other people, getting bylines placed with other peoples' names on them, and watching people on TV with my words in their mouths. I'm finally at a point where I can start to share my own words, my own story, with my own name attached.

But it's scary.

Writing for other peoples' bylines is a form of protection. It's a way to share ideas without having to endure the worst insecurities of posting on the internet with a female name.

I get ready to hit Publish on my next post. My mouse hovers over the button.

"What if they call me a bitch?" I wonder.

A quiet, knowing voice responds, "Don't worry, they already have."

/32

Stuck: How Leaders Get Trapped, and How to Save Yourself

Growth, executive expectations, and a pun for good measure

> Johnathan

Almost every startup sets the same trap, and almost every founder and executive falls for it. I certainly did. And I've watched friends and colleagues do the same.

It's not immediately obvious that you're trapped. A lot of the symptoms just feel like the challenges of scale. In a sense, that's all they are. But the way they act on you makes you put off solving them. And the more you put them off, the deeper you get stuck.

How many of these feel true to you?

→ **Your meetings are too big.** They mix people from a variety of departments and seniority levels. They are often twelve to fifteen people wide or more. You defend this as being about a diversity of input and avoiding top-down groupthink. Whatever the reason, the result is slow and ineffective meetings, which leads to slow and ineffective teams.

→ **Your calendar is a mess.** Where you spend your time tells me what your priorities are.[1] Yours should be the long-term health and direction of the business. Instead your day is full of ad hoc conversations and deep dives into details. You're extremely available to your people for quick questions, but nobody can get your undivided attention when they need it. You never have the kind of time needed to make big, thoughtful decisions unless you hide in a meeting room or a coffee shop.

→ **Your bus factor is too high.** What if you got hit by a bus? Would people be left in the lurch? That's always true for execs, and doubly so for founders. But you make it worse for yourself. Your team *could* step into broader ownership and accountability, but they never have to. You're always right in there. That's great for alignment but awful for organizational growth and a direct barrier to scale.

→ **Your company isn't where it needs to be.** There are other people who can sweat the details, but few who can set direction. You are doing good work, but it's work others should do. And the result is that you aren't where your people need you most.

Feeling trapped yet?

Stuck

The trap is sticky for two reasons. First, it sticks because all the symptoms are interrelated. You could put a cap on meeting size,[2] but without trusted delegates you'll still need to attend every one.

And because you attend them, it's a place for people to get your uninterrupted time and so they'll all want in. And now your meeting is too big again. You can't fix any one thing without fixing all the things, and *that feels so big.*

The second reason the trap is so sticky is that escape feels like failure. Having an assistant feels haughty. Telling people they need to book time with you feels arrogant. Asking "Is this presentation ready for *me?*" or "Does this meeting actually require an *executive* to be present?" feels so pompous. So you tell yourself that those things are the trappings of ego, and you stick to what has worked in the past.

Only it's not working now, or you wouldn't still be reading this.

Fallacy

There's a popular concept bouncing around these days called the stack fallacy.[3] Maybe you've heard of it. The stack fallacy observes that companies consistently underestimate how hard it is to build products higher up the technology stack. Mobile OS vendors think apps are easy, and they're wrong. Database providers think CRMs are easy, and they're wrong. That sort of thing.

To unstick yourself, you need to recognize that a related thing happens with leaders in an organization experiencing rapid growth. Because we are hilarious people, let's call it the *stuck fallacy.* 😉

The Stuck Fallacy: Growing startups consistently undervalue the support roles and structures present in larger organizations.

I understand that you don't want to be a pampered corporate stereotype. No one does. When you were small, the wholesale dismissal of operational supports felt *lean and agile*. But you're bigger now. Staying stuck in that way of thinking is now the biggest thing slowing you down.

Escape the Trap without Hating What You've Become

Growth happens when you let go of the behaviors and attitudes that no longer help you. You can keep to your values but recognize that they need different expressions as your team gets bigger. Let me give you an example.

I know a founder whose real concern as his organization grows is that he remain accessible to the team. He's a great strategic thinker but doesn't want to just sit in a leather chair *strategizing* all day. He wants to be where his people are. He feels the importance of having the founder voice be present and approachable. And he's drowning.

For him, the way to express that value is to take lots of meetings and get involved early in every process. The result is that he often sees early, junior work and feels the need to make it better. He answers questions other people can answer and solves problems other people can solve.

My advice to him was to admit how big his organization has become, and what that means for his role. To give away his Legos, as Molly Graham says.[4] He doesn't have to give up being accessible, but he might have to put some structure around it—Friday hosted lunches, or scheduled skip-level one-on-ones, or town hall sessions. He shouldn't stop being involved in developing work, but it's fair for him to ask if it's ready for his attention.

It isn't sustainable for hundreds of employees to expect daily affirmations from the founder. He knows it. I think mostly he needed permission to say so without feeling like a pretentious ass.

This Generalizes

Your trap might look different than his. You might be hung up on a different word than accessibility. Maybe *performance*, or *mission*, or *hustle*. It's still a trap if you're trying to do all the heavy lifting on your own. You're still stuck if your systems haven't grown as your team has.

I have worked with people who overcorrect on this point. Who feel that being an executive entitles them to conspicuous privilege, and more still in secret. Who *impose* their status instead of reluctantly accepting it. I'll be honest, I find them much harder to love.

But the rest of you need to cut yourselves some slack. It's hard work doing what you do. It's okay to set some boundaries about how your time gets spent. It's okay to invest in process and people support to let you focus on the right things. It's more than okay. It's your new job.

/33

Maternity Leave:
An American in Canada

On motherhood as a startup exec, maternity leave as an expat, missing work as a recovering workaholic, and the perils of mama group imposter syndrome

> Melissa

As I write this, I've been on maternity leave for a few months. It's been both incredible and strange to be away from work to get to know the tiny human I made. Incredible because did I mention I helped make an actual human? And strange because this is the longest stretch I haven't worked since I was 18.

Let that sink in for a second. This is the longest I've been off of work in my *entire adult life*.

That's not burnout bustage talking. At least, I don't think it is.

I love what I do. I'm one of the few people I know who went to school and studied what would eventually be my career. I have worn a bunch of different hats and had many different roles, but all in the same industry, and almost all focused on emerging companies and/ or nascent tech. I still wake up most days excited to work in tech.

The idea of taking a year off didn't feel like an opportunity to run away from a dead-end job. Nor did I harbor a secret desire to do a job search in Month 11 in hopes of quitting after mat leave. **I was genuinely excited to spend time with my kid, but I was also genuinely excited at the prospect of my return.**

* * *

In the moments of quiet calm when the baby is occupied with the potato masher (currently her favorite toy), my thoughts drift. I find myself thinking about my American mama counterparts. I think about my sister and my sister-in-law. I think about my closest friends from childhood. And I wonder how different my experience of motherhood and careerhood would be if I were in the U.S.

In Canada I can take up to a year of maternity leave and still return to my job. The government provides Employment Insurance; it's not a salary replacement, but it helps cover some costs while I'm off. I am fortunate to live in a country with such progressive family leave policies.

In the U.S. it varies, but mat leave is six to twelve weeks and much of that requires stockpiling your vacation time and then cashing it in. Let's take a moment and all laugh out loud at the idea that newborn care has anything to do with vacation.

I recognize that being able to stay home with my daughter like this is something our family can do while many other households cannot. But in Canada I'm not the exception. The norm is for people to take the full year.

When I told people that I thought I might go back before the year mark, I was suddenly well outside the norm for Canadian mamas.

"What do you mean, you don't think you'll take the full year?"

"You know you'll never get this time back again. They're only babies once."

"I can't imagine not having had the full year with my kids."

"Work will be there when you get back. Your team will be fine without you. They'll figure it out."

I hand picked my mat leave contractor. I knew my team would be fine without me. They would learn new things from a seasoned leader whom I trusted to run the show in my absence.

I had dropped my office hero complex years earlier. I already knew that startups were dynamic, living, breathing things. They grow, they break, they bleed, they stitch back together in different configurations, they heal.

I didn't need my work to need me. I needed *it*.

◆ ◆ ◆

Most people find that if they can survive the first three months of a newborn, things start to get easier from there. That wasn't my experience. And the weird thing about babies is that we automatically assume two unrelated three-month-olds have anything in common.

If you walked into a room of one hundred 50-year-olds from around the world and were asked what those people all had in common, you'd look for the super broad generalizations. They were all born. They all breathe air. They will all die. And that might be the end of your guesses. At no point would you make assertions about their temperament, sleep patterns, education, brain development, or food preferences. Because that's an insane thing to do for humans, who are all special little snowflakes.

That we do it for babies as a cohort is bizarre. That we do it for babies by gender ("Oh, that's just how little boys *are*") is also weird.

Anyway, three months was not our turning point of awesome. That turning point was still several months away, so while my mama friends and the people in my baby groups were getting high off of procreation and delighting in their bundles of joy, I was, well, I was really tired.

"Isn't motherhood just the most amazing/magical thing ever?"

"Don't you just love her so much?"

"Don't you just want to stare at her while she sleeps?"

"Do you ever just check on her to make sure she's still breathing?"

• • •

Canadians have an expression that I didn't know until I got here. They talk about "making space." It took me a while to get the hang of it the idea, but it's basically *leaving conversational room for the other person to express their ideas, to dissent, to disagree.* As far as I know, Americans don't have an equivalent cultural concept. As a group, we are quick to dissent, vocal when we disagree, and not shy about expressing ourselves.

After months of being on the receiving end of unadulterated mama bliss, I suddenly found I needed a lot of space. There was no room to say I was tired. There didn't seem to be space for anything that wasn't a Stepford-like enthusiasm for the aforementioned miracle of creating a small human.

I was staring down an entire year of silently suffering through baby groups where they changed the lyrics to "Humpty Dumpty" so that it would have a happy ending and skipped verses of "You Are My

Sunshine" because they were sad began to feel insufferable. I felt the walls closing in on me.

I missed work. More than that, *I missed who I was at work.* I missed feeling smart and competent and on top of things.

This was the first time in my life I felt like I was failing in every direction and couldn't just outwit the problem. And it was compounded by the sense that there was no appropriate outlet for my mat leave imposter syndrome.

"Isn't motherhood just the most amazing/magical thing ever?"

It's great. I'm not sure why my teeth are gritted like Thurston Howell the Third right now, but it's great. Really. Really. Great. Swearsies.

"Don't you just love her so much?"

Sometimes. Is "sometimes" an okay answer?

"Don't you just want to stare at her while she sleeps?"

Honestly, if she's sleeping, I want to be sleeping. Or showering. *Staring* also starts with an *s* and ends with *-ing* but no, that is not what I want to be doing.

"Do you ever just check on her to make sure she's still breathing?"

It hadn't even *occurred* to me that that was a possibility.

• • •

When my daughter was born, I'd already been stepparenting my big kid for four years. Though I was a first-time bio parent, it wasn't my first at bat for caring, feeding, nurturing, and loving a small human. I suspect this colored my experience of first-time motherhood in that it was both a new and a not entirely new experience at the same time. This also put me a bit outside the baby group discussions around how to co-parent with your partner for the first time, how to leave the kid with a babysitter, why dirt and germs are an important part of your kid's diet, etc.

So much of what was hard about those early months was feeling alone, like I was the only mom who missed work. Or, worse, that something was wrong with me because I didn't have the insta-bliss my friends reported.

At about five months, we found our turning point. It wasn't overnight, but I can look back and say that while we still had ups and downs, the overall trend line started to improve.

With more sleep, I could see that I was in the wrong baby groups. I quit the ones that changed lyrics to provide universally happy outcomes. Bit by bit, I found my mama tribe. We'd go on long walks. We'd drink strong coffee. We'd talk about the good, the bad, and the ugly parts of caring for a baby. We'd say out loud that we were lonely. Or bored. Or tired. Or that we couldn't remember the last time we'd brushed our teeth or hair. Or worn an actual bra.

• • •

I had told work I to expect me back after six months. That was already double the amount of time off I could expect if I'd been in the U.S. Before my daughter was born, it was hard to imagine being off for longer than that.

I need to know this baby. I need to feel like I got to enjoy our time together and for the first four months, we could barely leave the house. I need more time. I want the summer. People in Toronto are at the cottage in August. The office will be quiet. I'll go back when the weather turns.

I had already made my decision.

I called my head of HR.

There was no guilt. There was no stress. There was no shame. My head of HR did not hesitate. She was supportive and understanding. She let me set my terms and do what made sense for me and my family.

◆ ◆ ◆

In my faraway gaze, when the baby is happily banging the potato masher on the top of her Exersaucer, I think about how that conversation would have gone if I were still living in the U.S. I remind myself that parental leave varies by company and that empathy varies by HR person.

But when I'm honest with myself, I let my brain acknowledge what my heart already knows: **I'm lucky to be a mom in Canada.**

Over the past few months, I have frequently looked at my partner and said, "It's just the most magical thing that we made a human. Isn't she amazing?!"

I stare at her while she sleeps and I check to see if she's breathing (all via baby monitor so as not to wake her—I'm not a total chump).

And when our girls are laughing together, a big knot wells up in the middle of my chest and I am physically overwhelmed by how much I love them.

Motherhood isn't just one thing. There isn't just one way to do it. To assume so is as ridiculous as walking into that room full of 50-year-olds and expecting them to have anything in common.

/34

Family Planning While Working in a Startup
A short guide to the awkward waters
of procreation and the workplace
> Melissa

Ughomgwtf

I've been back at work post–mat leave for a few weeks now. I'm deep in ramp mode and trying to get back in the flow of things at the office. So much has shifted since I've been gone, and while the surroundings and faces are familiar, the context has changed. I'm spending a lot of time learning and understanding the current state of the business.

While I love catching up with folks over coffee, I've been mindful to focus my time in the office and put social calls on the back burner.

So I'm surprised when I looked at my calendar and find that a social call had somehow slipped through. I notice it at 9 a.m.; the coffee was for 10 a.m. Something tells me I should keep this meeting.

I find myself sitting across from a woman I've met a few times professionally but don't know very well.

"How are you?" I ask. "I haven't seen you in a few months. What's new?"

"Well," she says, holding onto the last *l* a bit too long, "I'm starting a family."

"Congratulations! That's wonderful news!"

"It is, but I don't feel like everyone is reacting to it that way. People keep telling me I'm going to end my career."

I feel the red flush creeping from my earlobes to my cheeks. I'm not mildly irked: I'm deeply bothered by this, and my body is responding like I'm about to get into a fistfight.

She continues: "And it's not men who are saying this. It's senior women in tech."

Ughomgwtf.

She already knows I don't agree with whoever she's been talking to, so I'm cautious not to come out swinging.

Deep breath.

"I think you know this already, but I don't agree with the people who said that to you. There's so much wrong with that sentence, I'm not even sure where to start."

I take a sip of my tea and use the moment to gather my thoughts.

She doesn't need a lecture right now. That's unlikely to be helpful. But I want to beat this notion so far into the ground that whoever planted it in her head doesn't get any more undue airtime.

And it occurs to me that if she's sitting across from me, nearly in tears, struggling with how to talk about family planning in a startup context, she's not alone.

It can be scary stuff but *we need to talk about it*. We need startup employees, who regularly negotiate everything about their package on the way in, to feel like they can ask questions. This isn't limited to the interview process; this is about giving people a safe space across the board.

For anyone who has ever contemplated starting a family where one or both parents are working in a startup, this will be familiar.

Mentioning the Unmentionable

The problem with family planning is that the moment you ask about mat leave or pat leave, people know you're thinking about having a kid. They may not know if it's imminent (i.e., that you or your partner are pregnant), but they definitely know it's on your mind.

You are curious about family benefits before you take the new job but you don't want them to think you aren't serious. You worry that it might impact their willingness to give you an offer.

You haven't been at the job for very long. You hesitate to ask about maternity benefits, lest they think you were pregnant when you applied and feel duped for hiring you.

You've been trying unsuccessfully to get pregnant. You now have a bunch of medical appointments (not to mention costs) looming and you need to know what's covered. Rather than ask someone, you scour the company intranet for details.

Given the many reasons *not* to bring family planning up at work, how is anyone ever supposed to get good, clear counsel on this important topic? Add to that the fact that startups are notoriously light on HR, process, and benefits that are actually written down somewhere, and it's no wonder so many people are confused.

If you're a startup wondering what you can do to help, start by writing down your family leave and benefits packages. Post it somewhere people can find it without having to ask. Better still, include the information in your offer package materials for *all* new hires, regardless of age or gender.

Ambition and Procreation Are Not in Conflict

If you're ambitious in tech, the idea of your boss or your HR person knowing that you're thinking about having a kid or are about to have a kid can feel daunting.

You worry that once they know you're pregnant or thinking of getting pregnant, they will treat you differently. This worry isn't unfounded.[1]

You feel like being off will soften your skills, undercut your aspirations, and put the brakes on everything you've worked so hard to build.

You wear loose clothing and wait as long as possible to tell people at work that you're expecting. You don't want to miss out on contributing to the big projects that hit after your due date.

The young woman I spoke to in that room loves what she does and doesn't want to slow down the trajectory of her career. Her concerns are real. The tension she feels between her hard-won career and her baby is not helped by the chorus of voices tell her it's either-or.

Like a Boss

Everything that's hard about family planning in a startup as an employee is at least doubly hard as a boss.

You worry that you won't be taken seriously, that your team won't respect you, and that they will all develop short-timer syndrome once they hear you are expecting.

You know that the moment you communicate change, the natural response is for folks to wonder "What does this mean for me?" If you're still getting used to the idea of creating another life yourself, this is probably the last thing on your mind.

You want to be able to walk into those conversations, communicate happy news, and have that be it. But that's not what it means to be a boss or an exec in a startup context. It's not that people won't be happy for you; it just means you need to brace for the change response from your boss, your peers, your HR team, and particularly your direct reports.

One thing you can do to prepare for those discussions is to think about it in advance. Do you anticipate taking leave? Do you have a sense of what that might look like (knowing that every baby is different and those plans are highly subject to change)? Have you thought about how your team will run in your absence?

The most concerning part for many senior people is the idea that these decisions will be made without their input, that there won't be space for them to come back after leave, or that major changes will happen while they're gone.

I found that having a plan made me feel better. It meant that when I walked in to finally tell my team that I was expecting, I had answers for them about what to expect while I was expecting. There were major changes while I was out, but helping design my mat leave coverage put my mind at ease. It allowed me to shut off Slack and email and focus on my family.

8 a.m. Is the New 8 p.m.
Many parents credit their kids for helping cut through the noise.

When I shared the news about my pregnancy, I had a fellow startup exec mama tell me, "You think you were efficient before. Just wait."

Months later, I'm conducting a meeting via Skype with the baby asleep in a Moby Wrap on me and I'm making a PB&J sandwich off camera. That exec's words come rushing back to me and I smile.

Juggling startup life and parenthood is an exercise in ruthless prioritization and focus. Somewhere between my first coffee and my daily sprint to the parking garage, a whole bunch of things have to get done. My hard stop at the end of the day is a *hard* stop.

If you can't fathom startup life without the quiet of the late-night grind, I've got news for you: 8 a.m. is the new 8 p.m.

The kids get up so friggin' early. They have no respect for weekends. They barely respect dawn. But it means I'm in the office for nearly two hours before the first scrum kicks off, drinking my coffee, triaging my day, and optimizing for a timely departure. I leave work and head into the post-work hustle that is kiddo pickup, dinner prep, and bedtime routines.

Starting a family will change your career. It will change how you engage with work. It will for sure change how you view after-hours networking events. But let's be really clear here: different is not the same as dead.

To the young woman at the start of this chapter (*you know who you are*):

You will be amazing. You will be more productive than you ever thought possible. You will bring a new energy to your work because you know that at the end of the day, you're going home to spend time with a tiny person you helped create.

You think you were efficient before. Just wait …

/35

Are You Too Smart to Work Hard?
The one about bullets and quicksand
> Johnathan

Some of the best parts of my time at Mozilla were the moments of brilliant humility. We had assholes, to be sure, but there would be these moments...

Twenty people sitting around a conference table during an all hands. Each of them brilliant—brilliance like I've rarely encountered before or since. The people in that room could reinvent the internet from sand and germanium on up if humanity ever misplaced the one we had. And every one of them in that room convinced that they were the dumbest one there.

It felt like we could outthink any problem. I loved those moments.

And, like so many nice-feeling stories I write about in this book, they were quicksand and I didn't see it.

Bullets

I was in one of those moments the first time I read Ben Horowitz's "Lead Bullets" essay. It's a story born out of Netscape, Mozilla's origin myth, and still I almost skipped it. I don't love war metaphors in business; they often feel callous and gross. But somehow this essay got through.

It kicked me in the gut. It lit something up that I had been feeling but hadn't labeled. If you haven't read it yet, go.[1] It's not long. I'll wait.

What hurts about that essay is that I, and most of Mozilla, had gotten addicted to silver bullets. I don't blame anyone in tech for falling into the same trap. Our industry is built around *disrupting*. We *think different*. It infuses our language and our value systems because it's an incredibly powerful tool set.

People rag on *disruption* as an overused word, and I get that. But holy shit our industry *really does* blow up some stuff. It's so rewarding to fix an entire *class* of problems. It reaffirms our belief that there are silver bullets out there if we're smart enough to look for them.

Never mind that we push out other important stuff to get those wins.[2] Never mind that it's impossible to appropriately size or plan around those insights. Never mind that they aren't as frequent as they seem and our examples are drenched in survivorship bias. They happen, and they feel great.

The Easy Way Isn't

Is your organization lured by the same temptation? Have you fallen into the same quicksand? It's easy enough to figure out:

Imagine a problem comes up that would be labor-intensive to fix manually. You discover that thousands of new accounts haven't been tagged with the right attributes. Or you have an API change that's going to break a whole ecosystem of third-party apps. How do you respond? How does your team approach the problem?

Everyone will, of course, look first for the obvious smart fix. Can we auto-deduce the missing tag? Can we shim the old API? Let's say there isn't a quick fix. Now what? **This is where it gets really interesting.** This is where the ground sinks beneath you.

Many companies, *smart companies full of smart people*, will keep looking for a way to think themselves out of it. They'll look for a *very, very* long time. At small scales, this is the running joke of engineering. Every programmer has a story about the time they spent longer automating a task than it would take to just do it.[3]

But some organizations spend *years* on this stuff. They spin up teams for it. They find a glimmer of hope, announce that a fix is on the way, and then delay over and over as they discover that the problem goes deeper. They are addicted to outthinking. The sunk costs are devastating.

You don't *have* years to spend on this stuff.

The Only Way to Win Is to Not Play

The organizations that dodge this trap share a crucial adaptive trait. After that initial sniff test to see if there's a quick way out, these groups **stop chasing after an elegant solution and just do the grunt work.** That's it. They see the ground shifting under them as they start to contemplate a brilliant way across, and they stop it dead. They sense that it's not safe. And they're right.

Need to re-tag those accounts? Grind it out through a mix of partial, unsatisfying fixes and good old-fashioned repetitive labor. Need a way to port those third-party apps? Send some emails. See which ones you can convince to rewrite on their own, and volunteer your own developers to help fix the rest.

Do the hard work. Put the problem to bed and move on. This isn't news. I'm not the first to suggest that grinding works. It's what Paul Graham was on about in "Do Things That Don't Scale,"[4] and he wasn't the first, either. Neither was the lead bullets essay. But I still meet plenty of folks stuck in quicksand, so it seems the message bears repeating.

3% Wins

Not all problems get the grunt-work treatment. Sometimes incomplete solutions are more damaging and you do need to fix things the right way. **A sign of a healthy team is that it should be easy to cite examples of each.** But many teams, particularly those with engineer founders, strongly prefer "elegant" solutions to grunt work. And it's where you can win.

While your competitors look for silver bullets, push through. You pay an upfront cost in ugly labor that your competitors won't. But with your team no longer distracted, every day that goes by is a little incremental win, 2% or 3%. For a big, really distracting problem, more.

Those wins add up. They compound. There is no greater miracle than compound interest in your favor. And there is no greater foe than compound interest pitched against you.

Your team will get better at finding these wins. It's a different mindset to see grunt work and think "How can I grind this out efficiently?" instead of only ever asking "How can I obviate this problem altogether?" The 3% wins build up faster. And more of them are 5% wins.

The silver bullets do happen. Occasionally you find a 100% win. Once in a *very* long while you will find a 10x lift, a 1000% win. They're worth looking for, at least some of the time. But the team doing the hard work and putting up those little wins every day is a lot more reliable. You can predict those marginal wins. You can plan for them. You get to the point where you can rack up a few 2% and 3% and 5% wins every week. Do the math over months and years. I'll give you a hint: It's far better than 1000%.

/36

Go Faster: How to Move with Confidence
Getting unstuck, letting go, and making the impossible possible

> Melissa

At home, my little kid is learning to walk. For anyone who's watched this process, it manages to be remarkably slow and fast all at the same time. I suppose the same could be said of all parenting milestones, but learning to walk is particularly interesting because once mastered, few of us can recall what it felt like to learn.

I find myself stuck on this idea of *how we go from tentative half steps to moving with confidence*. How we transition from this place of nervous energy, where we're looking around to see if there's anything to grab onto, and get to a point where we make bigger, more audacious moves. Where we let go of the first hold before we're attached to the next.

The question keeps showing up in some form or another, gnawing at me, echoing at home and then popping back up throughout the day.

How might we move with confidence?

I'm watching my little person tackle this uncertainty. She scoots along the edge of the coffee table. She lets go and wavers back and forth like a little drunk person. She grabs for the table, catches her balance, and then half steps toward me, falling face first into my arms.

It is not graceful. It is not smooth. It is choppy and uncertain and unstable. But she has reached her destination. And she did it by being brave.

We cheer.

◆ ◆ ◆

How is it that this happens and most of us don't remember it?

And how remarkable, still, that this turns out to be the framework for lessons we will learn many times across the course of a lifetime.

Instability. Fear. Failure.

Followed by more trying. Deliberate practice, slow at first. And then more, bit by bit.

Until finally. Movement.

Uncertain, ungraceful, unstable, but no longer an impossibility.

Back at the Office

Back at the office, I'm in classic startup form. I'm asking a team of people to think differently, to stretch themselves, and to do work that's never been done before.

They like this in theory. It's what they signed on for. If they wanted predictable and well-worn paths, they wouldn't have picked a startup. So there's some self-selection forces already at work. It's a good team and they're eager.

But I'm not asking for theory. I'm asking them to make their best effort based on incomplete information. To assert without all the facts. To take semi-informed risks. And to adjust as new information becomes available.

In practice, it's a lot like watching my kid scoot along the edge of the coffee table. Not because my coworkers are kids—because the fundamental question is the same:

How might we move with confidence?

But We Don't Know Anything

Walk into any modern company today and you'll find people paralyzed by what they don't know. These people struggle to get started because the universe of options seems so vast, so daunting, so overwhelmingly infinite.

But when you ask a few questions, what you find is that most folks actually have a pretty good idea of where they want to end up. They can even articulate a bunch of the stuff that needs to happen along the way.

In my corporate communications days, I did an ungodly amount of messaging work. The starting point was always the same: An overwhelmingly blank canvas. A clean whiteboard. A blinking cursor in a shared Google Doc. A wall full of those giant sticky notes that some genius at 3M came up with.

People freeze. They want to make the first words perfect. They get so stuck that they can't write anything down.

Instability. Fear. Failure.

"Okay, let's use all the *wrong* words. That will help us get to the *right* words."

Followed by more trying. Deliberate practice, slow at first. And then more, bit by bit.

Slowly, we write some things up on the board, we clarify, refine, find the threads.

Until finally: movement.

We start to make sense of it. We erase, rewrite, and shuffle things around until everything found its place.

Uncertain. Ungraceful. Unstable.

At the end of a session, we've used only what was in the room to fill the board. We go out into the world and test those assumptions—with press, on web copy, on blog posts, with potential investors. And we integrate changes back into the master messaging doc.

It's no longer an impossibility.

We have this idea that we don't know anything, and it gets in the way of us moving. It can paralyze a team. And from a place of stuckness, it can be *really* hard to get unstuck. But if you can articulate the 20% in which you are confident, you're already part of the way there.

With that 20% under your belt, you can better assess the relevant bits, you can make strategic bets, you can accept, assess, and take informed risks. You can share your working assumptions, you can invite discussion and feedback.

You can align your team around the vision, and from there, you can finally start to get some wind behind your sails.

You can not only move—you can move *fast*.

Making the Impossible Possible

At first, it's pulling up. Maybe it happens once. Maybe it's a fluke. Maybe you're on the phone with a grandparent at the time and you shriek with delight that the little kid just pulled up. And maybe the grandparent doesn't entirely get why this is so monumental.

It's okay. Sometimes it takes a while for true genius to be appreciated.

This is what it looks like in the early stages.

Unrecognized by some. Celebrated by others. Simply ignored more often than not.

Trying, falling, trying again, maybe not for some time, but then again. And again. And again. Mastering at first on steady, reachable things, with shaky knees and unstable footing.

Followed by pulling up on any solid surface above or below until standing…on solid ground.

Finding stability, only to lean, reach, stretch, and then finally, finally, finally,

…let go.

/37

Are Strong Values Destroying Your Company?
Some thoughts on why, and what to do about it
> Johnathan

Values are great. You should definitely have some.

Great leaders are clear about their values. That clarity attracts talent and improves results. If a vision is the company's reason for being, values are what govern how we get there. Apple is clear about theirs. So is Tesla. Google has replaced "Don't Be Evil" with "You can make money without doing evil." Less inspiring, maybe, but clear just the same. These companies don't always live up to their values. But they aspire, and I like aspiration.

So anyhow, *yay, values!*

There's No Such Thing as a Free Lunch

Here's the thing, though. Every value you commit to has the power to ruin you. The more forcefully you proclaim them, the more you set yourself up for failure. You can prevent that failure, but only when you recognize the forces behind it. Two things make this difficult:

→ **Every value eventually grows a vicious downside.** It's usually not the living, breathing values that hurt you. It's the ossified values that you one day discover have grown malignant.
→ **Organizations have an allergic response to value change.** When a leader tries to mitigate the downsides of a value or its interpretation, people feel like the value is under attack. Values are moral concepts, so the response to this change isn't strategic or reasoned; it's outrage.

I want to talk through a few examples here. Just a few, though. I will miss some of your values, but don't be fooled into thinking you're exempt.

1. We have a flat structure; anyone can talk to the executives about their ideas.

More than 90% of startups I talk with have some version of this value. It's got a lot going for it. It distinguishes us, as an employer group, from banks and other megacorps competing for technical talent. It supports the need of early-stage startups to learn constantly and to gather in as many inputs as possible. And it flatters founders and other executives who believe they are accessible and down to earth.

As your organization grows, though, it starts to hurt. The number of interactions grows, and your leadership team gets pulled into hundreds of tactical and procedural conversations. As a result, they will start to be selective about who they make time for, creating informal power structures and cliques. Even still, they are too time-sliced to elevate. They don't have the time to really think through the strategic, long-term direction of the organization. Which is *their job*. No one feels good about how this is going.

At some point, it tips. Your executives get assistants and closed-door offices. Everything starts to happen through calendars. New hires see this structure and assume that executive attention is precious and special. This sets off an allergic response among long-time employees. They talk about how *corporate* things are now. It saps morale. Your values statement becomes an ironic joke for these people who see the current state as hypocrisy.

Sound familiar?

2. We hire the best and brightest. We encourage honest and open discussion to get to the best ideas.

I see this kind of value more often when dealing with leaders who come from academia. Personally, I'll take strength of group execution over individual smarts, but I don't fault folks who want to have smart people working on big ideas. When you assemble a critical mass of brilliance in your organization, really breakthrough things become possible. And nothing attracts smart people like the opportunity to work with other smart people in a culture that values *smart*.

As your organization grows, though, it starts to hurt. The PhD style of discussion that develops is a crucible. New ideas are torn apart and burned down to see if they can withstand critique. The value placed on *smart* creates an incentive for competition, and so people start to get torn apart and burned down, too. The people who can stand this kind of *honest and open* start to look a lot alike: mostly men, mostly with enough privilege to have advanced education that trained them in this form of conversation.

At some point, it tips. Salaries climb so that you can retain your increasingly entitled brain trust. The flight of what little diversity you had prompts leadership to bring in more HR support and soft skills training. In response to this rise in *political correctness*, employees become more aggressive. Disagreement, even requests for respectful communication, become a mark of dumbness. Anyone else with a good idea either keeps it to themselves or works on it in private for as long as possible.

Am I getting warm?

3. We're not here for the money— we're here for the mission.

This is a value every nonprofit explicitly takes on, but many for-profit organizations trumpet some version of it, too. Some do it to appeal to investors, customers, employees, or the media, but many of them really do believe it. Either way, it works. The best people are motivated by things beyond money. The focus on mission lets your people be creative. It gives the media and your investors a great story to tell on your behalf. Yes, the organization has to pay its bills and please stakeholders, but it *feels good* to tell a mission story. It feeds your soul.

As your organization grows, though, it starts to hurt. There are lots of ways to advance the mission that vary wildly in their revenue potential. Your mission is unique, so most of the metrics you use to measure success are idiosyncratic and hard to calibrate.

Even with mission as a North Star, alignment between teams suffers because there's no backstop or reality check. Staff who underperform are insulated from consequences because their role is so mission-focused.

At some point, it tips. While your team is chasing unfocused definitions of *mission*, your burn rate grows. You start to measure initiatives based on their contribution to revenue, or at least *sustainability*. You have all-hands meetings and spend an immense amount of time to explain the obvious: that our mission can't happen without cash. The old guard sees this as a moral failure.[1] Some folks get it, but a deep schism forms between idealists and pragmatists. The idealists quietly call themselves the only *real* members of the organization.

Ever been in this kind of organization?

And so forth

I gave you three examples, but the list goes on. Years before I wrote this, Shanley Kane wrote her phenomenal "What Your Culture Really Says,"[2] and her points are all still true. Spend the $10 if you haven't read it yet.

It's easy to spot the double-edged values once you start looking. Because all values are double-edged. Every value statement draws a line through the world and says, "We want to be on this side, not that side."

We want to be like these people, not those people.

But it's silly to imagine that *those people* have no wisdom to add. It's juvenile to think that your way is completely superior and gives up nothing of worth. Of course you're giving things up. Good values just let you be clear about which trade-offs you'll make.

Yay, Values?

I *still* think values are great. I'm happiest at companies that are clear about them, that help new team members learn them, and that support everyone in living by them. My challenge to you, when you are writing your organization's values, is just to *think them all the way through*. Here are a few gentle shoves, in case they help:

→ **Define most of your values in the positive space.** It's a small difference, but it matters. An org that says "We care a lot about X" has a much easier time introducing Y and Z than one that says, "We care about X more than Y." Or worse, "We're about X. Not Z." The clarity of the negative space is useful, but only for things you're ready to kill the company for, rather than accept.

→ **Ask yourself the real cost of each value and whether you're willing to pay it.** I'd rather you have fewer values and stand behind them, than to see you list off twenty and slowly whittle them down as you realize how expensive they are. If you think the trade-off for a given value is negligible, you're not thinking hard enough.

→ **Watch out for reinterpretation.** As your team gets larger, everyone will have their own spin on what your values mean. As a leader, listen for those and make sure they are still pointed the right direction. In particular, new folk may redefine your values in a more polarized way. Correct them fast. Values can evolve as you grow, but you should not passively let misinterpretation become canon.

When in Doubt, Call It Out

A good value should fit in a tweet, but I'd rather you get it right than get it pithy. It's okay to add explicit interpretation and notes. The benevolent grace of the World Wide Web has given us all **Headers** and *Body text*; use them. If your header is Mission Above All Else, have the body text talk about how reliable revenue streams are critical to the ongoing success of that mission.

Spell out what you're thinking as you set your values. Repeat those interpretations whenever you teach or revisit those values. And when a value paints you into an impossible corner, admit it and have the conversation head on. It's good for you, and essential for your team. Do it well and you might make it out alive.

/38

Idle Work and
Busy Hands
How to Maintain Workplace
Momentum in Uncertain Times
> Melissa

Somewhere between the end-of-year planning you did late last year and the first few months of this year, you have an *oh shit* moment. It's not that the planning was useless—it's that the market has moved and your operating context has shifted.

You suddenly find yourself in the midst of a major strategic shift. You can keep going in the same direction, but your internal road map is littered with Trouble Ahead signs. There's a pivot brewing.

The best startup pivot stories come from companies that were on the brink of certain death. The team makes a last-ditch effort, throws caution to the wind, and emerges victorious...just before everything falls apart.

The retelling always feels quite fast, the pre-pivot moment like a mere blip in the company history. While the majority of startups don't make it to a post-pivot history, the ones who do fast-forward this part of their corporate lore.

The truth is that while the need to pivot may be obvious, the internal process typically takes a while. There's a gap between when senior leaders first sense the need for change and when the entire organization has retooled their efforts around a new set of objectives.

Between Two Points

Point A is the recognized need for a change. Point B is the moment that change has been realized across the organization. The road from A to B is a bumpy one, and sometimes the car breaks down along the way.

Management presses pause on all ongoing efforts. The first quarter finishes and the leaders sequester themselves to work on second-quarter planning. The start of the second quarter comes and goes with no update. Staff stop being able to book the big conference rooms. Leaders across the organization stop showing up for meetings. The organization is now a full month into the second quarter with no stated goals or objectives.

People keep coming to work, but their anxiety levels rise. The major projects that seemed so critical back in January are in purgatory. They may be cut, or they may continue on under the new strategy but, without an update from the leadership team, languish. They limp along without sign-off from key stakeholders. The key stakeholders aren't sure if the work even matters.

Without a clear idea of what work is in scope for the upcoming quarter, no one sees the point in running themselves ragged. The teams start to slow way down...just in case.

Uncertainty Reigns

While bosses are working on the pivot, line staff are wondering what's happening. With free time, they *begin* to guess.[1] The lack of oversight on their current work makes them nervous. They begin to suspect that their work is not important. They haven't had a one-on-one with their boss in several weeks. Something is up.

Am I gonna get laid off? Should I start looking for a new job? I guess it's time to update my LinkedIn profile.

It's pretty easy to understand how we got here. There's no point in starting work that might be the wrong work. It's best to put down current projects and wait for next steps. This makes a lot of sense on the face of it—no one wants to do a bunch of work on something that will later be thrown away.

Managers of high performers tell themselves there's nothing worse for morale than working hard on things that don't matter. But there *is* one thing worse for high performers than working on things that don't matter, and that's working on nothing at all.

After a month or two of this, the top performers have started returning calls and emails from the recruiters who pinged them months ago. No one is pushing hard on internal deadlines. People aren't sure about the direction of the business or the value of their work, so they get busy with other things, namely, interviewing and getting the hell out of there.

Top folks start to peel off—one or two people, at first. More follow. Former staff are offered recruiting bonuses to help their new employers fill open roles. The diaspora grows.

The sequestered leads pick their head up from time to time, but a cohesive strategy is still several weeks (months?) away.

What was once a well-oiled machine grinds to a halt.

Just Keep Swimming

Nobody likes busy work. It has a well-deserved and awful reputation. The words alone are enough to make most people cringe.

Johnathan tells a story about one of his first jobs, in which he carried boxes of legal folders from one side of a warehouse to another. Once the boxes had all been moved, their contents were thrown into a shredder.

In one of my first internships, I printed reports off of the internet and put them in neat, color-coded binders. I then put the binders on a bookshelf, where they were promptly forgotten.

It's comical to think about these moments now, twenty years later. I've spent a lot of time as a boss. I wonder how many of my former interns have their own stories about an activity that seemed like a colossal waste of time in retrospect.

Yet despite its bad reputation, there are moments when busy work is precisely what the doctor ordered.

Remember those two points we talked about earlier? The recognized need for change and the moment when the change has been realized? In the space between is a lot that is out of your control. But there are several things you can do, even if you don't have the full strategic picture of what comes next:

1. **Say something.** You won't have the answer about what comes next until well after your people need it, but you can say something and have it change later or you can tell them nothing at all. It's up to you. Just keep in mind that in the nothing-at-all version, your people will likely make up a worst-case scenario that's more dire than the one you're actually in.

2. **Keep moving.** You may not know what the post-pivot world entails, but you should know the work that has to get done to keep the lights on while you figure it out. Center your efforts there. People want to feel like they are contributing to mission-critical work. The stuff that has to get done anyway isn't busy work in the classical sense, but it *is* work that will keep people busy. And it will give you some much-needed air cover to sort out the strategic direction of the business.

3. **Adjust course.** Changing course is so much easier than getting rolling again after a cold stop. The effects on morale of months trudging along in a low-impact, low-effort world are real. If you can keep people moving, you can keep the basic frameworks intact about how they show up and work together to achieve common aims. If you let those fall apart, getting moving again is going to be much harder.

Pivots happen. Strategic changes happen. Most grown-ups can understand this and are able to roll with the punches. Where people struggle is when the path ahead is uncertain and there's nothing they can do.

Give them something to do.

/39

What to Do When
It All Falls Apart

How it felt to be part of Mozilla's
biggest crisis, and what happened next

> Johnathan

The hardest month in my life as a leader was in the spring of 2014. I was VP Firefox at Mozilla. I was one of the senior leaders during Brendan Eich's ascent to, and resignation from, the role of CEO. And it was how I came to find myself talking to most of the company with no script, in a moment of crisis.

I'm not going to pick off all the old scabs. I'll give you the short version, in case you genuinely don't know. If you need to know more, Stephen Shankland got a lot of it right in his piece a few months after it all happened.[1] Stephen usually gets it right, and there should be more journalists like him.

The Short Version

The short version is this: Brendan cofounded Mozilla with Mitchell Baker more than a decade earlier. After a year-long CEO search failed to find a good fit, Brendan stepped into the CEO role. The scrutiny that comes with a role like that quickly brought up a donation he'd made in support of California's Proposition 8, a move to oppose same-sex marriage. The donation is a matter of public record and had already come to light years earlier. **But the CEO is under a different level of scrutiny.**

And so all hell broke loose.

Progressives online demanded he resign. Some Mozilla employees joined in. The tech press spent a few days on it, but then the national and international press got hold of it. Mozilla was the subject of morning talk shows and nightly news. People used words like *embattled*.

By Day 4, a friend of mine said to me, "It's already over and he just doesn't know it yet." Until that moment, I didn't know it, either.

Mozilla started to get rage through every channel. My impression is that Brendan and his family got much more. Our staff's families started to ask why they worked for a homophobic organization. There were boycotts, and opportunists tried to tie their own marketing campaigns to Mozilla's damage.

I remember the video call when Brendan told the senior staff he was going to resign. I remember how tired he looked.

Having become a *cause célèbre* for one side of the debate, we came under heavier attack after he left. The weapons of the activist right were unloaded on anything Mozilla. Even today, Brendan's name is used as an incitement to anger. We'll get angry book reviews because of this chapter. The hate follows any discussion of those days.

I don't agree with Brendan's politics, if you care to know. I can't imagine voting to tell my friends their marriages count for less.

It's a morally repellent idea to me. But I have love for Brendan just the same. And I remember how those days felt. Disagreeing with him didn't make any of it easier.

And that's the *short* version.

Here's How It Feels

When your organization is in crisis, you expect it to feel like panic. But it doesn't: it feels hollow.

Everyone comes to work but no one works. There's no music playing in the office, and there's no chatter in the kitchen. Instead of code or designs on people's screens, it's news articles. It's Twitter.

I've talked with the leaders of a lot of organizations, and this feeling is consistent. Layoffs, founder trouble, money trouble, lawsuits...whatever it is, and I'm sure it's awful, the hollow will feel the same. Nothing louder than whispers. And occasionally, tears.

The Call

I think the day Eich's resignation hit was a Thursday. I sent an email to the Firefox team letting them know that I'd be in my video room if anyone wanted to talk.

Two people joined right away. Someone joined from our Mountain View office in a room with half a dozen others. Then Berlin. Then Vancouver. Over the next few minutes the tiles of faces filled up until we hit the limit of what Vidyo could display. But the chimes as new people joined kept sounding. And in Mozilla's Toronto office, the room filled.

People didn't really know what to ask at first. They just wanted to be where other people were. When the questions did come, they were scattered. People didn't, by and large, *have* questions yet. They just *felt terrible* and wanted not to.

For my part, I didn't really have answers, either. As a spokesperson, you get accustomed to knowing questions before they're asked. You're briefed on each reporter you speak with. You have a set of points you're trying to get across. Candor and clarity help make an interview connect, but you still never lose sight of key messages.

There were hundreds of people on that video call, and I didn't have any key messages. I don't know where I would have gotten any. I didn't even know who my boss was, exactly.

Three things saved me that day. In the months that followed, the feedback I got was that these three things were enough to bring several people back out of the crisis to a productive place:

→ **Already-built trust.** When your organization is suffering and they don't believe you or believe *in* you, it's too late to start earning it. That call happened because people felt like I would be straight up. If they didn't believe that, they never would have showed up in the first place.

→ **Honesty, honesty, honesty.** It is so much more important in crisis to be honest than to be polished. People asked me how I felt personally, and I told them. I felt tired. I felt sad, and disappointed, and unsure about a lot of things. I suspect that's not *executive orthodoxy*. But they all felt it, too. Trying to tell them anything else would have been foolish. Honesty is the only way to lead in crisis. And that honesty gave me permission for the next thing.

→ **Clarity (and honesty, honesty, honesty) about what comes next.** You won't know, of course. Not all of it, at least. But you'll know some things. The access that comes with being a leader means you might see the next few weeks more clearly, at least. On the call I said, "Everyone will still get paid for their work. We'll keep shipping Firefox. I'll work with Mitchell and Chris until we decide on a new CEO. None of that changes, and it's the same for those of you in other parts of the organization. For today we're going to process this news, and maybe tomorrow too. But on Monday we have work to do, and I'm going to expect you all to show up for it."

This may seem obvious to you. Obviously payroll doesn't stop when the CEO leaves. Obviously it's good to be honest. Obviously it helps to have concrete work and timelines to focus yourself. Obviously.

But nothing is obvious in a crisis. It's not obvious to your team that the company will be around in a month. It's not obvious that you'll still be there, either. And for you, as a leader during crisis, it's not obvious that you want to be. Everyone gets tunnel vision. So stick to the basics. State the obvious.

What it feels like to stay in an organization post-crisis and rebuild is a different chapter that I haven't yet written. But in the moment, you are a leader in an organization that needs you. Take a deep breath. Figure out how you really feel. And then get on the call.

/40

Is It Worth Your Time to Be Excellent?

You may experience some discomfort on this ride

> Johnathan

You're not where you're supposed to be.

You're not a failure. You're actually doing well. You have a way you present yourself at parties that sounds pretty impressive. You have a *narrative*.

But you're not better at the stuff that makes you great than you were three years ago. Maybe you call those feelings "imposter syndrome" when they show up. Maybe you keep busy with lateral moves and jumping companies. Either way, you're running up against the same walls.

I've met you. In fact, I bet you think this song is about you.

The Secret

I'll give you the secret. I'll tell you the thing that knocks down those walls and unlocks a whole new growth path for your professional life. I know it will, because I lived it. I know it will, because once you know what to listen for, you hear almost every success-ful leader point to it.

What's more, it's so powerful, it will also totally alter your personal relationships. You'll be a better partner and a better friend.

And here's the zaniest piece of all: **I'll tell you, and most of you still won't do it.** You can send this to other people, and they won't either.

Isn't that wild?

Anyhow—here it is. You won't like it.

Be vulnerable.

What the Hell Does That Mean?

Be vulnerable.

I understand that it sounds like self-help snake oil. I promise that's not my intent. The truth is that being vulnerable is hard. *Really* hard. But, past a certain point, it's the only way you get better.

Before Malcolm Gladwell made the 10,000 hours thing so cool that it became uncool again, it was a pretty neat paper.[1] The authors *did* find that most world-class experts took about 10,000 hours to get there; that part is true. But not just *any* 10,000 hours. Being alive and present for 10,000 hours doesn't count. Plinking away at the piano for 10,000 hours or writing bad poetry for 10,000 hours or shooting free throws for 10,000 hours doesn't make you world class.

Neither, by the way, does natural talent. Natural talent only lets you outrun the amateurs. Look at someone like Michael Phelps—from what I can tell, that guy is part fish. I feel like every four years the U.S. media has a new set of articles about how his arms are a bit longer than average and his lung capacity is larger than most. In the next few years I suspect we'll learn that he has gills and swims upstream in the spring to spawn. But I'm here to tell you that without an incredible training and coaching regimen, Phelps wouldn't even be a contender. He'd win every local swim meet and be destroyed at the Olympic level.

The only way to get to world-class level, the thing that the original study authors *actually mean* when they talk about 10,000 hours, is by something they call *deliberate practice*. It's 10,000 hours of watching your tapes and watching other people's tapes. It's 6 months adjusting a single form or working a single piece. It's asking, constantly, "Where am I messing up?" and "How can I get better?" "Who does this better than I do and what can I learn from them?" Imagine 10,000 hours of that. Not an hour, or 10, or 100. It's exhausting. It's why being a world champion is hard.

Be Vulnerable

I don't swim or run or climb for a living. I manage teams. I lead people, and I try to help them build products people love. Maybe you do something similar. I'm still working on my 10,000 hours. And whenever I stall, I find that the same thing gets me out of it.

Where am I messing up? How can I get better? Who does this better than I do, and what can I learn from them?

I don't know what it's like to be an Olympian, but for me those are uncomfortable questions. Sometimes my narrative takes over. I try to listen and make serious-looking faces, but I also look for the ways to get out of hearing something I don't want to learn about myself. I have natural talent around people—I can often pass the amateur tests without taking it too much to heart.

But on my good days, which come more frequently with practice, I am vulnerable. I am open to the prospect that it will hurt to learn that I'm still messing up. And sometimes it does hurt. I didn't make a call when my team needed me to, or I made a call too quickly, or I made a straight-up dumb call. I didn't listen or, worse, I listened selectively. As soon as I hear this stuff, I know how true it is. And I feel like an idiot. Those are the days when I get better.

Meh?

Maybe you think this is all a bunch of navel-gazing, self-indulgent garbage. Certainly no small part of my own success comes from privilege that has nothing to do with how *vulnerable and brave* I am. 😊 The very ability to be vulnerable at work is privilege—many folks can't afford to, and part of my job is to reverse that wherever I can. It's one of the places I know I still have a lot to learn. And what I have learned so far has come mostly from the generosity and patience of people who have had to work much harder to get where they are than I did.

But for some of you, those first couple paragraphs sting. **You're stalled and you know it.** You're leaning on your natural talents and your position in life instead of doing the hard work to get better. You tell others, and maybe even yourself, that you *are* looking for feedback, that you *are* vulnerable. In fact, you're the first to volunteer how awful you are at things, partly as faux humility, partly as genuine insecurity. Yeah, I see you.

But honeys...I'm not asking you to beat up on yourself more. Stop that. I'm asking you to *work*. What's the common pattern for your last three failures, and what are you going to do about it that isn't just deflection? Who are you asking for help and coaching, and how well can they see through your narrative? How hard do they help you push?

Anyhow, that's the secret. And if you go back and read the interviews with great leaders and world experts and championship athletes, you'll hear it over and over again. I hope you'll grab onto it.

Because it's killing us to see you stuck like that.

Notes

CHAPTER 1 HOW FUCKED UP IS YOUR MANAGEMENT?

1. Valve, *Handbook for New Employees* (Bellevue, WA: Valve Press, 2012), www
   .valvesoftware.com/company/Valve_Handbook_LowRes.pdf; Philippa Warr,
   "Former Valve employee: 'It felt a lot like high school,'" *Wired UK*, 9 July 2013,
   www.wired.com/2013/07/wireduk-valve-jeri-ellsworth/.

2. Chris Dannen, "Inside GitHub's super-lean management strategy—and how
   it drives innovation," *Fast Company*, 18 Oct. 2013, www.fastcompany.
   com/3020181/inside-githubs-super-lean-management-strategy-and-how-it-
   drives-innovation; Alex Wilhelm & Alexia Tsotsis, "Julie Ann Horvath
   describes sexism and intimidation behind her GitHub exit," *Techcrunch*,
   15 Mar. 2014, techcrunch.com/2014/03/15/julie-ann-horvath-describes
   -sexism-and-intimidation-behind-her-github-exit/.

3. Michael Lopp, "How to recruit," 6 Sept. 2016, randsinrepose.com/archives/
   how-to-recruit/.

CHAPTER 3 YOU WON'T BRILLIANT YOUR WAY OUT OF THIS

1. Caroline Simard, Andrea Davies Henderson, Shannon K. Gilmartin, Londa
   Scheibinger & Telle Witney, *Climbing the Technical Ladder: Obstacles and Solutions
   for Mid-level Women in Technology* (Michelle R. Clayman Institute for Gender
   Research, Stanford University & Anita Borg Institute for Women and Technology,
   2008), gender.stanford.edu/sites/default/files/Climbing_the_Technical_Ladder.pdf.

2. Danny Schreiber, "Gary Vaynerchuk of VaynerMedia," Big Omaha Video Series, *Silicon Prairie News*, 13 May 2011, siliconprairienews.com/2011/07/big-omaha-video-series-gary-vaynerchuk-of-vaynermedia/.

CHAPTER 5 THAT TIME YOU FAILED TO FOLLOW UP ON DIVERSITY

1. Feminist Technology Collective, Resources, *Model View Culture*, modelviewculture.com/resources.
2. Susan J. Fowler, "Reflecting on one very, very strange year at Uber," 19 Feb. 2017, www.susanjfowler.com/blog/2017/2/19/reflecting-on-one-very-strange-year-at-uber.
3. Mitch Kapor & Freada Kapor, "An open letter to the Uber Board and investors," 23 Feb. 2017, *NewCo Shift*, shift.newco.co/an-open-letter-to-the-uber-board-and-investors-2dc0c48c3a7.
4. Olivia Solon, "Crazy at the wheel: Psychopathic CEOs are rife in Silicon Valley, experts say," *The Guardian*, 15 Mar. 2017, www.theguardian.com/technology/2017/mar/15/silicon-valley-psychopath-ceo-sxsw-panel.

CHAPTER 6 SOME GARBAGE I USED TO BELIEVE ABOUT EQUALITY

1. Caroline Fairchild, "This 'sad' advice a male VC just gave to women in tech couldn't be more wrong," LinkedIn, 29 Sept. 2016, www.linkedin.com/pulse/sad-advice-male-vc-just-gave-women-tech-couldnt-more-wrong-fairchild.
2. Anil Dash, "Not a 'good guy,'" 24 Feb. 2015, anildash.com/2015/02/not-a-good-guy.html.
3. Bourree Lam, "When resumes are made 'whiter' to please potential employers," *The Atlantic*, 23 Mar. 2016, www.theatlantic.com/business/archive/2016/03/white-resume-diversity/475032/.
4. Mitch Kapor & Freada Kapor, "Dear investors: So you want to take diversity seriously (Part 1)," *Medium*, 18 Feb. 2016, medium.com/@mitch_freada/dear-investors-so-you-want-to-take-diversity-seriously-part-1-777972b5450c.
5. Sarah Sharp, "Closing a door," 5 Oct. 2015, sarah.thesharps.us/2015/10/05/closing-a-door/.

6. Lauren Parker, "The the list of books men must read before messaging me about feminism," *Athena Talks*, 5 July 2016, medium.com/athena-talks/the-list-of-books-men-must-read-before-messaging-me-about-feminism-3894594bf311.

7. Dash, "Not a 'good guy.'"

CHAPTER 7 THE TECH *MECHITZA*

1. Shanley Kane, "'Fuck you, I got mine': Women in tech for the patriarchy," *Medium*, 11 oct. 2013, quoted 5 Mar. 2014 at femininethings.tumblr.com/post/78724246500/fuck-you-i-got-mine-women-in-tech-for-the.

2. Tracey Ross, "The unsettling truth about the tech sector's meritocracy myth," *Washington Post*, 13 Apr. 2016, www.washingtonpost.com/news/in-theory/wp/2016/04/13/the-unsettling-truth-about-the-tech-sectors-meritocracy-myth/.

CHAPTER 9 PRIVILEGE, ILLEGAL INTERVIEWS, AND BURNING CURIOSITY

1. For Canada, see José Gonzalez, "8 types of illegal interview questions and how to avoid them," TalentEgg, 16 July 2010, talentegg.ca/incubator/2010/07/16/8-types-of-illegal-interview-questions-and-how-to-avoid-them/; for the U.S., see Patrick Allan, "The most common illegal job interview questions you should watch out for," *LifeHacker*, 26 May 2016, lifehacker.com/the-most-common-illegal-job-interview-questions-you-sho-1706238105.

CHAPTER 10 YOUR DIVERSITY PROBLEM ISN'T THE PIPELINE'S FAULT

1. Vivian Hunt, Dennis Layton & Sara Prince, "Why diversity matters," McKinsey & Company, Jan. 2015, www.mckinsey.com/business-functions/organization/our-insights/why-diversity-matters.

2. Marianne Bertrand & Sendhil Mullainathan, *Are Emily and Greg More Employable than Lakisha and Jamal? A Field Experiment on Labor Market Discrimination*, NBER Working Paper No. 9873 (Cambridge, MA: National Bureau of Economic Research, 2003), www.nber.org/papers/w9873.

3. George Desvaux, Sandrine Devillard-Hoellinger & Mary C. Meaney, "A business case for women," *The McKinsey Quarterly*, Sept. 2008, dca.org.au/app/webroot/files/file/gender%20documents/Business%20Case%20for%20Women%20Mckinsey%20sept08.pdf.

4. Stefanie K. Jonson & David R. Hekman, "Women and minorities are penalized for promoting diversity," *Harvard Business Review*, 23 Mar. 2016, hbr.org/2016/03/women-and-minorities-are-penalized-for-promoting-diversity.

CHAPTER 11 THE SECRET TO BETTER INTERVIEWS (AND MAYBE A BETTER LIFE)

1. Susan Wu, "Welcome to diversity debt: The crisis that could sink Uber," *Backchannel*, 2 Mar. 2017, https://backchannel.com/welcome-to-diversity-debt-the-crisis-that-could-sink-uber-df0165cccf77.

2. Biz Carson, "Google's infamous brain-teaser interview questions don't predict performance," *Business Insider*, 6 Oct. 2015, www.businessinsider.com/google-brain-teaser-interview-questions-dont-work-2015-10.

CHAPTER 13 BIG LIES, LITTLE LIES, AND THE CHEAT CODE TO A PROMOTION

1. Daniel Kahneman, "Of 2 minds: How fast and slow thinking shape perception and choice," excerpt from *Thinking Fast and Slow* (Farrar, Straus and Giroux, 2011), in *Scientific American*, 15 June 2012, www.scientificamerican.com/article/kahneman-excerpt-thinking-fast-and-slow/.

2. Amit Chowdhry, "Microsoft CEO Satya Nadella apologizes for comments on women's pay," *Forbes*, 10 Oct. 2014, www.forbes.com/sites/amitchowdhry/2014/10/10/microsoft-ceo-satya-nadella-apologizes-for-comments-on-womens-pay/.

3. Jen Agg, *I Hear She's a Real Bitch* (Toronto: Doubleday, 2017).

4. See, for example, modelviewculture.com.

CHAPTER 15 HOW TO NEGOTIATE LIKE A BOSS

1. Pascal Finette, "Follow up (or shut up)," 21 May 2013, read.theheretic.org/follow-up-or-shut-up-9d599a2a76e3.

2. Alison Griswold, "Paid in prestige: Why does the top editor of the *New York Times* make so little money?" *Slate*, May 2014, www.slate.com/articles/business/moneybox/2014/05/jill_abramson_new_york_times_salary_dispute_why_is_the_top_editor_paid_so.html.

CHAPTER 16 YOU KNOW YOUR PRODUCT TEAM IS FAILING. DO YOU KNOW WHY?

1. Ben Horowitz, "Good product manager/bad product manager," Andreessen Horowitz, 15 June 2012, a16z.com/2012/06/15/good-product-managerbad-product-manager/.

2. Andrew S. Grove, *High Output Management* (New York: Penguin 1995).

CHAPTER 19 UNLIMITED VACATION AND OTHER FORMS OF GUILT-BASED MANAGEMENT

1. Neal Ungerleider, "Kickstarter nixes unlimited vacation time for employees," *Fast Company*, 24 Sept. 2015, www.fastcompany.com/3051537/kickstarter-nixes-unlimited-vacation-time-for-employees; Jeanne Sahadi, "Tribune reverses course on unlimited vacation policy," CNN, 24 Nov. 2014, money.cnn.com/2014/11/24/pf/tribune-vacation-policy/.

2. Jonathan Chew, "Why unlimited vacation may sound better than it really is," *Fortune*, Mar. 10, 2016, fortune.com/2016/03/10/best-companies-unlimited-vacation/.

3. Jessica Leber, "Vacation policies you'll envy from companies you don't work for," *Fast Company*, 9 Mar. 2015, www.fastcompany.com/3043269/vacation-policies-youll-envy-from-companies-you-dont-work-for.

CHAPTER 20 HOW TO BE A BETTER LEADER IN 4 BADLY DRAWN CHARTS

1. Ze Frank, "My web playroom," TEDGlobal 2010, July 2010, https://www.ted.com/talks/ze_frank_s_web_playroom.

CHAPTER 21 THIS IS THE YEAR TO STOP GOSSIPING AT THE OFFICE

1. You might start at www.unslutproject.com.

CHAPTER 22 THE OPEN-FACED SHIT SANDWICH:

IMPROVEMENTS ON A CRAPPY ORIGINAL

1. Alina Tugend, "You've been doing a fantastic job. Just one thing…," *New York Times*, 5 Apr. 2013, www.nytimes.com/2013/04/06/your-money/how-to-give-effective-feedback-both-positive-and-negative.html.

2. Ken Blanchard & Spencer Johnson, *The One Minute Manager* (New York: William Morrow, 1982).

3. H.L. Mencken, "The divine afflatus," *New York Evening Mail*, 16 Nov. 1917.

4. Ben Horowitz, "Making yourself a CEO," Andreessen Horowitz, 17 Oct. 2012, a16z.com/2012/10/17/making-yourself-a-ceo/.

CHAPTER 26 WHY YOU SHOULD NEVER APOLOGIZE FOR CRYING IN THE OFFICE

1. Nick Clayton, "The hidden motives behind workplace perks," BBC, 10 Dec. 2014, www.bbc.com/capital/story/20141209-hidden-motives-behind-work-perks.

2. Westfesttv, "Snoop Dogg smokes out Twitter," uploaded 19 Jan. 2011, www.youtube.com/watch?v=MC1q5Dvgyjg.

CHAPTER 27 WHAT HAPPENS IN THE ROOMS WITH NO WINDOWS

1. Ijeoma Oluo, "But what if you're wrong? 5 rules for apologizing like a grownup," *xojane*, 4 Oct. 2014, www.xojane.com/diy/but-what-if-youre-wrong-5-rules-for-apologizing-like-a-grownup.

CHAPTER 28 YOUR NEW PROCESS IS NO SUBSTITUTE FOR GIVING A SHIT

1. Daniel H. Pink, *Drive: The Supposed Truth about What Motivates Us* (Riverhead, 2011).

2. See Chapters 15 and 10, and Michael Lopp, "The update, the vent, and the disaster," 22 Sept. 2010, randsinrepose.com/archives/the-update-the-vent-and-the-disaster/

CHAPTER 29 LEADERSHIP IS NOT ABOUT YOUR GOOD INTENTIONS

1. Valve, *Handbook for New Employees*.

2. "Emergency landing," Drucker Institute, 3 May 2013, www.druckerinstitute.com/2013/05/emergency-landing/.

CHAPTER 32 STUCK: HOW LEADERS GET TRAPPED, AND HOW TO SAVE YOURSELF

1. Pascal Finette, "Change your language," *The Heretic*, 15 Jan. 2013, read.theheretic.org/change-your-language-5de5a2841b80.

2. Vivian Giang, "The 'two pizza rule' is Jeff Bezos' secret to productive meetings," *Business Insider*, 29 Oct. 2013, www.businessinsider.com/jeff-bezos-two -pizza-rule-for-productive-meetings-2013-10.

3. Anshu Sharma, "Why big companies keep failing: The stack fallacy," *TechCrunch*, 18 Jan. 2016, techcrunch.com/2016/01/18/why-big-companies -keep-failing-the-stack-fallacy/.

4. "'Give away your Legos' and other commandments for scaling startups," *First Round Review*, Sept. 2015, firstround.com/review/give-away-your-legos -and-other-commandments-for-scaling-startups/.

CHAPTER 34 FAMILY PLANNING WHILE WORKING IN A STARTUP

1. Darlena Cunha, "When bosses discriminate against pregnant women," *The Atlantic*, 24 Sept. 2014, www.theatlantic.com/business/archive/2014/09/ when-bosses-discriminate-against-pregnant-women/380623/.

CHAPTER 35 ARE YOU TOO SMART TO WORK HARD?

1. Ben Horowitz, "Lead bullets," Andreessen Horowotz, 13 Nov. 2011, a16z. com/2011/11/13/lead-bullets/.

2. Om Malik, "Silicon Valley has an empathy vacuum," *The New Yorker*, 28 Nov. 2016, www.newyorker.com/business/currency/silicon-valley -has-an-empathy-vacuum.

3. Randall Monroe, "Automation," *xkcd*, 20 Jan. 2014, xkcd.com/1319/.

4. Paul Graham, "Do things that don't scale," July 2013, paulgraham.com/ds.html.

CHAPTER 37 ARE STRONG VALUES DESTROYING YOUR COMPANY?

1. Michael Lopp, "The old guard," 15 Oct. 2014, randsinrepose.com/archives/ the-old-guard/.

2. Shanley Kane, *Your Startup Is Broken: Inside the Toxic Heart of Tech Culture* (Model View Culture, 2014).

CHAPTER 38 IDLE WORK AND BUSY HANDS

1. Johnathan Nightingale, "If you hate the rumour mills, why did you build one?" *The Co-Pour*, 3 Apr. 2017, https://mfbt.ca/if-you-hate-rumour-mills-why-did-you-build-one-1a6aa4664ad9.

CHAPTER 39 WHAT TO DO WHEN IT ALL FALLS APART

1. Stephen Shankland, "Mozilla under fire: Inside the 9-day reign of fallen CEO Brendan Eich," Cnet, 13 June 2014, www.cnet.com/news/mozilla-under-fire -inside-the-9-day-reign-of-fallen-ceo-brendan-eich/.

CHAPTER 40 IS IT WORTH YOUR TIME TO BE EXCELLENT?

1. Malcolm Gladwell, *Outliers* (New York: Little, Brown, 2008); David Z. Hambrick, Erik M. Altmann, Frederick L. Oswald, Elizabeth J. Meinz, Fernand Gobet & Guillermo Campitelli, "Accounting for expert performance: The devil is in the details," *Intelligence* 45(2014):112–14, dx.doi.org/10.1016/ j.intell.2014.01.007; K. Anders Ericsson, Ralf Th. Krampe & Clemens Tesch-Romer, "The role of deliberate practice in the acquisition of expert performance," *Psychological Review* 100(1993):363–406, doi: 10.1186/1472-6920-11-101, graphics8.nytimes.com/images/blogs/freakonomics/ pdf/DeliberatePractice%28PsychologicalReview%29.pdf.

Gratitude

This book shouldn't be possible. Of all the things we might do while working day jobs as tech executives and raising two kids, writing a book is a ludicrous one to choose. While there are only two names on the cover, the full list of people who helped make this book happen would be longer than the actual book.

Making the Book Possible

Before we had a book, before we even had a blog, we had a living room. Much of what we've learned about management and leadership has come from our amazing colleagues and friends, and from the conversations over whisky about where we've all fucked up. Management isn't easy, and there aren't a lot of places where it's safe to talk about it, but we *need* those conversations. We need to be honest about it and vulnerable about what goes wrong, or each of us has to reinvent all the same mistakes. The trust in those co-pours has been the undercurrent for everything we've learned and everything we write.

Every co-pour is different, but they all start with the tink of glasses. To Deb and Rob, who keep us honest and don't let us blind ourselves with tech's optimism. They have been in tech longer than we have, get excited about it like we do, but give it no passes to misbehave or be less than it ought to be. To Cheryl, Amy, and Kristin. who come from outside of tech and help us remember that there is good in it even when it feels like a cesspool. To Kev, who brings honesty and self-reflection to every conversation. Everyone should have a Kev around to remind them to always hold themselves accountable first. And everyone should have a Lisa, with fierce loyalty and a strident insistence on holding others accountable for their piece, too.

To Christina, Ryan, Jessie, Erica, and Avery, our most enthusiastic champions. They can't imagine a world where we aren't wildly successful in all pursuits, even when we aren't certain ourselves. They bring boundless energy to any new idea we have, and want to be first on the team to help. All of them push us to work harder and think bigger, and if you have friends like this you, know how incredibly special that can be.

To the current and former HR people in our lives—Bonnie, Mihca, Jess, Anika, Debbie, Steph, and Dan. You folks are able to see it all now because you've seen it all before. You can spot the architecture of disaster setting up long before it hits. Thanks for understanding, for having cool heads during crisis, and for trying to hold the space for an entire organization.

And to all the other real life co-pourers out there. You have been with us from the start. We are forever in your debt. You are forever in our hearts.

Making the Book Better

Without the humbling generosity of those who taught us, it's difficult to say what kind of leaders or writers we'd be today. We say throughout this book that no one is born good at this stuff. We learned through failures, embarrassments, and many patient people we met along the way.

Outside of our parents (love you, Moms and Dads!), the first among those teachers were our own managers, leaders, and mentors. Not because they had all the answers, but because they were flawed leaders themselves, and knew it, and tried to do better anyhow. Melissa learned a great deal from Margit Wennmachers, Paul Kim, Crystal Hutter, and Allen Lau. Johnathan is so much better for his time with Chris Beard, Bob Lisbonne, and Ben Zifkin. We both come back to our conversations with John Lilly, Mitchell Baker, and Brendan Eich frequently. They're all referenced in these chapters, directly or otherwise. We are a product of the marks they've left on us.

We need to recognize the writers who have been doing this work longer than we have. It's *such a problem* that so many of the influential thinkers on leadership are old white men, but it remains true that we've learned a great deal from Andy Grove, Peter Drucker, and Patrick Lencioni. Michael Lopp and Ben Horowitz might not feel old yet, but their writing helped form our thoughts just the same. If you haven't read them, you should. You might not agree with them, but their work is canon.

In some ways the most impactful group in our growth as modern leaders has been the current generation of writers on the dynamics of power and privilege in work. The writers named in Chapter 6 are the ones doing the hard work right now to educate all of us, and you should be reading them, too: Ijeoma Oluo, Shanley Kane, Ashe Dryden, Saadia Muzaffar, Marco Rogers, Joanne McNeil, Kronda Adair, Anil Dash, Erica Joy, and Freada Kapor

Klein. Every one of them is quite findable online. Every one of them is uncomfortable to read sometimes. And every one of them has made us better.

Making the Book Happen

This book is adapted from our *Medium* publication (mfbt.ca), and it needs to be said that the thing Ev and the *Medium* team have built is really special. This book probably wouldn't exist without the writing tools they offer and the audience they helped us reach. We always felt (whether it was true or not, we'll never know) like we had fans inside the *Medium* team looking out for us.

A blog is not the same as a manuscript, though. The more we tried to turn one into the other, the clearer that became. Every word in this book is better because of our editor, Stephanie Fysh. When a new person edits you, you always get ready to disagree. You brace for how much you're going to feel pushed off of your voice. Stephanie's fingerprints are everywhere in this book, but you wouldn't know it, because she is a pro. She makes us sound like the smartest, clearest, and most concise version of ourselves. It's an easy thing to describe, but an awfully hard thing to do, particularly with multiple voices going back and forth. She should triple her prices.

Ingrid Paulson's design work inside and out then transformed what we wrote into an honest-to-god book. She understood us throughout the process. She made us print out early covers, tape them to books, and leave them around the house. We lined up office chairs like airplane seats to see how it felt to walk past one. We had short and direct conversations about interior paper color that concealed within them a fiery passion fueled by Cava. Cream, not white. A book, Ingrid told us, is a physical artifact, even when it's an ebook. You're holding a thing that she made, and we're so thankful to her for it. She should also triple her prices.

With Stephanie's and Ingrid's work, we'd have a really lovely book that we'd be proud of, and we'd have sold about a dozen copies. If you bought this book, if you've even *heard* about this book, it's because of the incredible advice we got from Ashleigh Gardner, our expert-on-the-inside at Wattpad, and the Page Two Publishing folks, Trena White and Zoe Grams. We really enjoy working with pros, and they are such consummate experts in every aspect of the publishing business that we left all our conversations buzzing. In the space of a few long phone conversations, they taught us printing, distribution, channel marketing, book launch mechanics, pricing strategies, and a hundred gotchas and secret tips we'd never have learned any other way. If you're working on a first book, you need them in your life.

And finally, thank you to Catherine Wright, the sleep coach. After we'd had seven months of sleepless nights with our youngest, Catherine came in and had her sleeping through the night in a week. There is no greater gift for the parents of a new baby than sleep. Our writing started shortly after that magical moment; without it, none of this would have been possible. If there are new parents in your life, be kind to them. And if you are a new parent, be kind to yourself. For all we talk about dealing with people in this book, those *tiny* people are a whole different ballgame.

This book is dedicated to our tiny people—less and less tiny by the day. We love you.

About the Authors

We're tech execs who have spent our careers running large parts of companies (product, engineering, data, design, marketing, PR, you name it). We've worked with several organizations you've heard of (Mozilla, IBM, Hubba, Edmodo, Wattpad, Creative Commons) and a bunch you haven't heard of yet.

These days we are the founding partners of Raw Signal Group, a management consultancy based out of Toronto, Canada. We continue to run The Co-pour, an online publication about management and leadership. And we continue to have people over to our living room for whisky when things aren't going well.

Melissa Nightingale has been a startup warrior since the first dot-com boom and has the branded T-shirt collection to prove it. She has held senior leadership roles in marketing, PR, and strategy at several fast-paced startups, including Wattpad, Edmodo, and Mozilla. Most of what she learned about writing came from her time at The OutCast Agency, SparkPR, and Edelman.

She moved to Toronto after more than a decade of working in senior tech roles in Silicon Valley and is gradually adjusting to seasons.